The
Cliché
Bible

8,400 Great Clichés For Sport Fanatics & Lovers Of Popular Expressions

-:|:-•:*'''''*•.•.-:|:-•**•-:|:-•:*'''''*•.•-:|:-

Compiled by
Richard & Lynn Voigt
I.M. Education Specialist

The Cliché Bible
8,400 Clichés For Sports Fanatics & Lovers Of Popular Expressions
© 2012 by RIVO Inc – All Rights Reserved!

ISBN-13: 978-1470021573
ISBN-10: 1470021579

First Printing, 2012

Printed in the United States of America

To Access More Powerful Marketing Tools Visit:

www.ActionHeadlines.com

www.Headlines.me

www.RIVOinc.com

Income Disclaimer

This book contains educational materials meant to inspire ways to promote personal ideas, products and services that may be appropriate to incorporate or use in or as a business strategy, marketing method or any other related personal or business advice that, regardless of the author's results and experience, may not produce the same results (or any results) for you. The authors make absolutely no guarantee, expressed or implied, that by using or following any of the ideas below that you will make any money or improve current profits, as there are several factors and variables that come into play regarding any level of achievement or success in said personal and/or business venture.

Primarily, results will depend on the nature of the product or business model, the conditions of the marketplace, the experience of the individual, and situations and elements that are beyond your control.

As with any business endeavor, you assume all the risk related to investment and money based on your own discretion and at your own potential expense.

If you intend to quote, copy, or use any content herein, in part or whole, it shall be the sole responsibility of you the individual to be mindful of all active and lawfully protected copyrights, trademarks, and/or services-marks, by conducting due diligence prior to said usage.

Liability Disclaimer

This book is strictly intended for educational purposes only and was intended to inspire the individual to create ideas of their own design. This book represents the views of the authors as of the date of publication. Due to constant changing conditions facing the information age, the authors reserve the irrevocable right to modify and update their opinions based upon changing conditions. While the authors have made a "good faith" effort to verify the accuracy of information within this book, the authors or their affiliates/partners do not assume any liability or responsibility for inadvertent errors, omissions, or inaccuracies. This book is not intended to be used as a legal guide or resource, nor are the authors attempting to render any legal, accounting, or other said professional services. If legal consultation or advice is required, the authors recommend the reader immediately seek the services of a competent professional for all legal or accounting advice. It shall be the reader's responsibility to be fully aware of federal, state, local or country laws that govern and affect said business transactions. Any slight of ethnicity, culture, gender, orientation, or existing organization as is any reference to persons or businesses, living or dead, is unintentional and purely coincidental.

Terms of Use

You are given a non-transferable, "personal use" license to this book. You cannot distribute it or share it with other individuals.

Also, there are no resale rights or private label rights granted when purchasing this book. In other words, it's for your own personal use only.

Now that all the legal stuff is out of the way, let's begin to have a lifetime of fun by applying, modifying, and customizing the following educational materials to help you creatively promote your own original ideas or marketing niche.

Now that the legal mumbo-jumbo is out of the way, it's time for you to enjoy the fruits of our labor.

The
Cliché
Bible

8,400 Great Clichés For Sport Fanatics & Lovers Of Popular Expressions

Compiled by
Richard & Lynn Voigt
I.M. Education Specialist

The Cliché Bible

The Cliché Bible is the most complete collection of Clichés ever assembled! This compilation contains a total of 8,411 Clichés, which includes 1,533 Sports Clichés and 6,878 Popular Expressions gathered especially for sport fanatics and connoisseurs of timeless popular expressions. From the beginning of time, expressions have been repeatedly popularized and passed down generation to generation leaving their mark, reflecting a lasting legacy of time and collective spirit of our global society.

A Cliché, whether serious or humorous, distills essential expressions going beyond truth as a point of conversation, insult, or reaction to a simple, complex, or profound and personal epiphany. Our DNA utilizes these expressions as an application connected to our daily life, even commonly reducing clichés into a new age of acronym apps.

This ultimate collection is a perfect instant reference guide for amateurs and   professionals alike. Whether you're an author, entrepreneur, business owner, novelist, ad writer, researcher, reporter, storyteller, journalist, historian, teacher, or student, this massive collection of popular cliché expressions can serve as a useful guide like no other.

Instead of struggling with writer's block, you can easily access powerful eye-grabbing clichés in a matter of seconds! Our inspirational collection will excite and inspire your creative juices with the full force of Niagara Falls.

Regardless of your interests, lifestyle, or profession; whether you're a sports fanatic or simply a lover of popular expressions, you'll love having this massive collection of Great Clichés at your fingertips.

SPORTS CLICHÉS

1	90% Of The Putts That Are Short Don't Go In		20	A True Tribute To A Great Athlete
2	A Balance Attack		21	A Week Off Will Do Them Some Good
3	A Couple Of Heavyweight Fighters		22	A Win Is A Win
4	A Driver's No Good Without A Pit Crew		23	A Win Today Snaps Their Four Game Losing Streak
5	A Flag There Usually Means Holding		24	A Win Tonight Will Force A Decisive Game Seven
6	A Game Of Contemplation		25	After A Goal
1	A Golf Ball Is Like A Clock Always Hit It At 6 O'clock And Make It Go Toward 12 O'clock But Make Sure It Stays In The Same Time Zone		26	After A Save
			27	After Blowing-Out The Other Team
			28	All-Star Break
			29	Always Takes A Lot Out Of A Car
8	A Golfer Has To Train His Swing On The Practice Tee, Then Trust It On The Course		30	Amazing 3 Day Rotation
			31	Amazing Control
			32	America's Pastime
9	A Good Sport Off The Field		33	An Incredible Season
10	A Lot Of The Faithful Are Heading For The Exits		34	An Unbelievable Season
11	A Major Leaguer		35	Another One For The Record Book
12	A Nickel Isn't Worth A Dime Today		36	Another Summer Has Past
13	A Perfect Match		37	Anything Less Than A Championship Is Unacceptable
14	A Real Nail Biter			
15	A Remarkable Machine		38	Anything Less Than A Win Is Unacceptable
16	A Sellout			
17	A Sports Legend		39	As Easy As Possible
18	A Tie Is Like Kissing Your Sister		40	As The Pendent Race Heats Up
19	A True Champion		41	Bad Calls Even Out Over The Course Of A Season

42	Baseball Banter
43	Baseball Is 90% Mental The Other Half Is Physical
44	Baseball Is Like Church Many People Attend But Few Understand
45	Baseball Is Won And Played Between The Lines
46	Bases Covered
47	Bear Down And Get The Job Done
48	Blown Call
49	Both Teams Are Playing At A High Level
50	Can They Pull Off Another Miracle
51	Can They Pull This Out
52	Can You Believe That
53	Carry The Ball
54	Carry The Team
55	Champions Aren't Made In The Gym But From Deep Inside
56	Champions Keep Playing Until They Get It Right
57	Classy On The Court
58	Coaches Who Win Get Inside Their Player's Mind And Motivate
59	Coast-To-Coast
60	Come Out Of The Gate Running
61	Come Out To The Ball Park
62	Concentrate On Hitting The Green And The Cup Will Come To You
63	Confidence Is Contagious So Is The Lack Of It
64	Count The Basket
65	Crunch Time

66	Daytona Always Takes A Lot Out Of A Car
67	Defense Wins Championships
68	Denver Draws First Blood
69	Despite The Losing Record
70	Despite The Losing Record, They're Just A Few Plays Away From Having A Perfect Season
71	Did My Eyes Really See What I Just Saw
72	Did We Just Witness His Last Game
73	Difference Between Impossible And The Possible Lies In A Person's Determination
74	Dime A Dozen
75	Do You Believe In Miracles
76	Do You Believe That One Folks
77	Do You Mean Now
78	Double Header
79	Down 2 Games To None
80	Drained It
81	Enjoy The Moment Everybody
82	Even God Has To Practice His Putting
83	Everybody's On The Same Page
84	Everyone Can Share This Moment
85	Everyone Counted Us Out Before The Season Started
86	Everyone Has To Be Held Accountable
87	Everyones Got A Tell
88	Fall Classic
89	Fast Break

90	Fatigue Makes Cowards Of Us All	119	Great Read By His
		120	Great Second Effort
91	Fly Through The Air With The Greatest Of Ease	121	Great Touch On That Pass
		122	Gut-Check Time
92	Focus On The Strike	123	He Adds A New Dimension To Their Offense
93	Football Is Like Life It Requires Perseverance		
		124	He Always Comes Through In The Clutch
94	For The Fun Of The Game		
95	Forget Your Opponents - Always Play Against Par	125	He Always Gives 100 Percent
		126	He Always Has His Team Ready To Play
96	Game Of The Week		
97	Game One Starts Now	127	He Beat Him Through The Five Hole
98	Game Over		
99	Game Postponed Due To Rain	128	He Brings A Lot To The Table
		129	He Bulls His Way For Extra Yardage
100	Get Back On Track		
101	Get In The Hole	130	He Bumped His Way Into The Field
102	Get Those Champaign Bottles Ready		
		131	He Called His Own Number
103	Get Up Get Up Get Outta Here GONE	132	He Can Break The Game Wide Open
104	Get Your Game On	133	He Can Bury The Three-Point Shot
105	Getting And Keeping Us In The Game		
		134	He Can Carry The Team On His Shoulders
106	Give Them A Lot Of Credit		
107	Give Them All The Credit	135	He Can Fill It Up
108	Giving Them A Good Thrashing On The Court	136	He Can Flat Out Play
		137	He Can Make Things Happen Out There
109	Go Get 'Em Next Time		
110	Goes The Distance	138	He Can Nail The Trifecta
111	Good Call By The Official	139	He Can Overpower The Hitters
112	Good Cut		
113	Good Teams Get Better Down The Stretch	140	He Can Play At The Next Level
		141	He Can Play On Sundays
114	Got To Give Them A Lot Of Credit	142	He Can Really Dish The Rock
115	Grand Slam	143	He Can Really Shoot The Three-Ball
116	Great Blocking At The Point Of Attack		
117	Great Individual Effort		
118	Great No-Look Pass		

144	He Can Really Sky For Those Rebounds
145	He Can Run Anytime He Wants I'm Giving Him The Red Light
146	He Can Spot Up For The Open J
147	He Can Take Over A Game
148	He Can Take This Team To The Promised Land
149	He Can Take You To School
150	He Can Tie It Up With One Swing Of The Bat
151	He Can Turn On The After-Burners
152	He Can Turn On The Jets
153	He Chased A Bad Pitch
154	He Couldn't Hit The Broad Side Of A Barn
155	He Couldn't Turn The Corner
156	He Crushed It
157	He Decided To Forego His Senior Season And Enter The Draft
158	He Definitely Left His Mark On The Game
159	He Does Things That Don't Show Up In The Stat Column
160	He Found The Twine
161	He Gets Stronger As The Game Goes On
162	He Gets The Most Out Of His Players
163	He Gives A Lot Back To The Community
164	He Gives Them Good Minutes Off The Bench
165	He Got A Good Jump
166	He Got A Step On The Defender
167	He Got Away With A Walk
168	He Got Hacked
169	He Got His Lap Back
170	He Got Out Of The Draft And Got Left Out To Dry
171	He Had A Man Wide Open Downfield
173	He Had Him Covered Like A Blanket
174	He Had To Check Off All Of His Receivers Downfield
175	He Had To Check Off His Receivers
176	He Had To Cut Back Against The Grain
177	He Has A Great Feel For The Game
178	He Has A Great Pair Of Hands
179	He Has A Killer Instinct
180	He Has A Linebacker Mentality
181	He Has A Lot Of Upside Potential
182	He Has A Low Center Of Gravity
183	He Has A New Lease On Life
184	He Has A Nose For The Ball
185	He Has A Passion For The Game
186	He Has A Rifle For An Arm
187	He Has A Tireless Work Ethic
188	He Has A Tremendous Passion For The Game Of Golf
189	He Has All Day Back There
191	He Has All Kinds Of Time

193	He Has All The Makings Of A Great One	225	He Hit A Rocket
194	He Has All The Time In The World	226	He Hit A Solo-Shot Back In The Third Inning
195	He Has All The Tools	227	He Hit A Towering Line Drive
196	He Has An Eternity	228	He Hit Him Right On The Numbers
198	He Has Blazing Speed	230	He Hit That Ball Squarely
199	He Has Blinding Speed	231	He Hit That One Right On The Screws
200	He Has Both Speed And Quickness	232	He Is Automatic
201	He Has Cat-Quick Reflexes	233	He Is Directing Traffic
202	He Has Elevated His Game	234	He Is Trying To Force The Ball
203	He Has Eyes On The Back Of His Head	235	He Just Did The Impossible
204	He Has Great Durability	236	He Just Gave Him A Little Bump To Let Him Know He's There
205	He Has Great Instincts		
206	He Has Great Lateral Mobility	237	He Just Threw Up An Air Ball
207	He Has Great Pocket Presence	238	He Knocked It Right Out Of The Ballpark
209	He Has Great Vision	239	He Knows What It Takes To Win
210	He Has Happy Feet	240	He Led Him Beautifully With That Pass
212	He Has Lightning-Fast Reflexes	241	He Left His Mark On The Game
213	He Has Speed To Burn	242	He Left The Field Under His Own Power
214	He Has The Complete Package	243	He Let's The Game Come To Him
215	He Has The Heart Of A Champion	244	He Lit The Lamp
216	He Has The Hot Hand	245	He Made A Complete U-Turn
217	He Has To Get Up And Down In Two	246	He Made The Right Decision
218	He Has To Wait For His Pitch	247	He Makes His Presence Known Out There
219	He Has Unlimited Potential	248	He Makes It Look Easy
220	He Hasn't Been Getting The Run Support	249	He Makes The Players Around Him Better
221	He Hasn't Ducked Anybody		
222	He Heard Footsteps		
223	He Hit A Bullet		
224	He Hit A Laser Shot		

250	He Moves Well For A Big Man
251	He Must Challenge His Players
252	He Must Regain His Past Form
253	He Nails The Buzzer Beater
254	He Needs To Bulk-Up In The Off-Season
255	He Plays Bigger Than His Size
256	He Plays With A Lot Of Emotion
257	He Plays With Reckless Abandon
258	He Provides Them With Instant Offense
259	He Put The Biscuit In The Basket
260	He Put The Lumber On Him
261	He Ran Into A Brick Wall
262	He Ran Out Of Real Estate
263	He Really Got A Hold Of That One
264	He Really Got His Bell Rung There
265	He Redefined The Game
266	He Reminds Me Of A Young _____
267	He Reminds Me Of A Young John His
268	He Reminds Me Of Another Guy Who Wore Number __
269	He Rumbled Down The Sideline For 30 Yards
270	He Runs A Squeaky-Clean Program
271	He Sent That One Into Orbit
272	He Shook Off Several Would-Be Tacklers
273	He Shoots A Rainbow Jumper

274	He Should Get An Academy Award For That Acting Job
275	He Silenced The Critics
276	He Stood Him Up On The Blue Line
277	He Tattooed That One
278	He Telegraphed That Pass
279	He Tested Positive
280	He Threw A Strike
281	He Threw Into Double-Coverage
282	He Threw That One Up For Grabs
283	He Threw Up A Prayer
284	He Thrives Under Pressure
285	He Took Something Off That Pitch
286	He Uncorked A Wild Pitch
287	He Understands His Role On This Team
288	He Wants This Fight
289	He Wants To Go Out On Top
290	He Was A Workout Wonder
291	He Was All Over That Pitch
292	He Was Blind-Sided
293	He Was Caught Napping
294	He Was Literally Run Over By A Freight Train
295	He Was Mugged
296	He Was On His Horse To Catch That One
297	He Was Really Clothes-Lined There
298	He Was Robbed
299	He Was Swinging For The Fence
300	He Went High To The Top Shelf
301	He Went Right Through Him

302	He Went Upstairs
303	He Won't Retire Until He Gets That Ring
304	He's A Good X's And O's Coach
305	He's A Real Gun-Slinger
306	He's Absolutely Livid On The Sideline
307	He's Audibilizing
308	He's Got A Step On The Defender
309	He's Spreading The Wealth
310	Heart Of A Champion
311	He'd Like To Have That One Back
312	He'll Be Buying Dinner For The Whole Offensive Line
313	He'll Have His Game-Face On
314	He'll Keep Playing As Long As He Can Contribute
315	He'll Know When It's Time
316	He'll Try To Tack On The Extra Point
317	Here's The Payoff Pitch
318	He's A Bench Warmer
319	He's A Blue-Chip Prospect
320	He's A Bruising Running Back
321	He's A Class Act
322	He's A Complete Player
323	He's A Contact Hitter
324	He's A Cutter And A Slasher
325	He's A Finesse Player
326	He's A Force On The Inside
327	He's A Franchise Player
328	He's A Freshman Phenom
329	He's A Future Hall-Of-Famer
330	He's A Good Guy To Have In Your Locker Room

331	He's A Good X's And O's Coach
332	He's A Great Role Model
333	He's A Gunslinger
334	He's A Highly Touted Freshman
335	He's A Leader On And Off The Field
336	He's A Legend In The Making
337	He's A Legitimate First Round Pick
338	He's A Lock For The Hall-Of-Fame
339	He's A Physical Player
340	He's A Physical Specimen
341	He's A Player
342	He's A Player From The John His Mold
343	He's A Project
344	He's A Projected Second Rounder
345	He's A Proven Winner
346	He's A Pure Shooter
347	He's A Real Competitor
348	He's A Real Gun-Slinger
349	He's A Real Throwback
350	He's A Rookie Sensation
351	He's A Scrappy Player
352	He's A Serious Student Of The Game
353	He's A Speed Merchant
354	He's A Steady Player
355	He's A Steal In This Round
356	He's A Streaky Shooter
357	He's A Talented Young Freshman
358	He's A Tough Out
359	He's A Tough, Hard-Nosed Player
360	He's A True Winner

13

361	He's A Warrior
362	He's A Wily Veteran
363	He's A Winner In The Bigger Game Of Life
364	He's A Work In Progress
365	He's A Youngster Who Bears Watching
366	He's Absolutely Livid On The Sideline
367	He's All About Winning
368	He's All Heart
369	He's All World
370	He's Always Been A Big Brother To Me
371	He's An All Star
372	He's An Ambassador Of The Sport
373	He's An Explosive Player
374	He's An Icon In This Town
375	He's An Impact Player
376	He's An Integral Part Of Their Offense
377	He's An Unselfish Player
378	He's As Good A Player As There Is In This League
379	He's Automatic
380	He's Been Feeling It
381	He's Been Perfect From The Charity Stripe
382	He's Been Playing Steady Between The Pipes
383	He's Been Quiet So Far
384	He's Been Relegated To The Bullpen
385	He's Been Riding The Pine
386	He's Been Roughed Up In His Last Four Outings
387	He's Been The Story Of The Game
388	He's Been The Subject Of Trade Rumors
389	He's Been Their Spark Off The Bench
390	He's Been Unconscious
391	He's Being Groomed For A Future Starting Job
392	He's Being Shopped Around
393	He's Built Low To The Ground
394	He's Calling It The End To An Illustrious Career
395	He's Capable Of Going The Distance
396	He's Career Is On The Line
397	He's Definitely A First Round Pick
398	He's Directing Traffic
399	He's Done So Much For The Game
400	He's Finally Getting His Due
401	He's Finally Playing His Natural Position
402	He's Getting Shelled
403	He's Going To Be A Great Quarterback
404	He's Going To Be Happy With That
405	He's Going To Be Stripped Of His Medals
406	He's Going To Re-Write The Record Books
407	He's Going To Set The World On Fire
408	He's Gonna Feel That One On Monday
409	He's Got 30 Homers On The Year
410	He's Got A Bad Wheel
411	He's Got A Bright Future In This League

14

412	He's Got At Least Another Season In Him	438	He's Overdue To Break One
413	He's Got Class Both On And Off The Field	439	He's Past His Prime
		440	He's Pin High
414	He's Got Good Mechanics	441	He's Pitching A Gem
415	He's Got Ice-Water In His Veins	442	He's Pitching Lights Out
		443	He's Poetry In Motion
416	He's Got The Batters Eating Out Of His Hand	444	He's Pure Looney Tunes
417	He's Got The Skills	445	He's Really Been In The Groove
418	He's Got Them Headed In The Right Direction	446	He's Really Been In The Zone
419	He's Had A Hall-Of-Fame Career	447	He's Really Coming Into His Own
420	He's Had An Up And Down Season	448	He's Really Throwing Some Heat
421	He's Having A Career Year	449	He's Really Whipped Them Into Shape
422	He's Having A Monster Game	450	He's Seeing The Ball Well
423	He's Having A Whale Of A Game	451	He's Seen Enough
		452	He's Silenced All The Critics
424	He's In A League Of His Own	453	He's Silenced All The Naysayers
425	He's In A Slump And He's Pressing	454	He's Slow Getting Up
		455	He's Some Kind Of Player
426	He's In The Greatest Shape Of His Career	456	He's Spreading The Wealth
427	He's Legit	457	He's Still Pitching A Shutout
428	He's Lost A Step Or Two	458	He's Still Playing Like A Kid
429	He's Making A Charge On The Back Nine	459	He's The Best Player Never To Have Won A Major
430	He's Never Missed A Game	460	He's The Best Player You've Probably Never Heard Of
431	He's On The Dance Floor		
432	He's On The Roster Now	461	He's The Consummate Team Player
433	He's On The Trading Block		
434	He's On Top Of His Game	462	He's The Epitome Of A Great Student-Athlete
435	He's One Of The All-Time Greats	463	He's The Franchise
436	He's One Of The Best In The Business	464	He's The Glue That Holds This Team Together
437	He's Only Played Sparingly This Season		

15

465	He's The Heart And Soul Of This Team		489	His Fastball Is Really Working For Him
466	He's The League's Most Underrated Player		490	His Presence Bodes Well For The Future
467	He's The Only Player Left From Their Championship Days		491	His Stock Is Rising
			492	His Telegraphed That Pass
468	He's The Real Deal		493	His Threw A Strike
469	He's The Stalwart Of Their Defense		494	His Threw That One Up For Grabs
470	He's The Unsung Hero On This Team		495	Hitting One Home Run After Another
471	He's Their Elder Statesman		496	Hopefully They Can Steal One On The Road
472	He's Their Field General		497	Hot Shot
473	He's Their Go-To Guy When The Game's On The Line		498	How About That One Folks
			499	How On Earth Did He Ever Pull That Play Off
474	He's Their Playmaker		500	I Believe His Ball Has Found Water
475	He's Their Role Player		
476	He's Their Spark Plug		501	I Did Not Knowingly Or Intentionally Take It
477	He's Their Workhorse		
478	He's Trying To Force The Ball		502	I Didn't Really Say Everything I Said
479	He's Trying To Pitch Out Of A Jam		503	I Don't Want To Point Fingers
480	He's Turned Out To Be The Ironman Of The Game		504	I Have High Expectations For This Team
481	He's Usually A Sure-Handed Receiver		505	I Knew I Was Going To Take The Wrong Train, So I Left Early
482	He's Walking Rather Gingerly		
483	He's Washed Up As A Player		506	I Know Deep In My Heart I've Done Nothing Wrong
484	Hey It's Only A Game And A Great Game At That		507	I Made A Wrong Mistake
			508	I Never Blame Myself When I'm Not Hitting I Just Blame The Bat
485	His Ability To Do That Is Just Uncanny		
486	His Attitude Is A Question Mark		509	I Question Their Shot Selection
487	His Called His Own Number		510	I Take A Two Hour Nap, From One O'clock To Four
488	His Career Is On The Line		

16

511	I Take Full Responsibility For This Loss	532	I'm Excited About This Opportunity
512	I Take The Blame	533	I'm Going To Give It My Best Shot
513	I Think It's Time To Call It A Day	534	I'm Going To Spend More Time With My Family
514	I Tip My Hat To Them	535	I'm Happy I Could Make A Contribution
515	I Want To Thank You For Making This Day Necessary	536	I'm In A State Of Shock
516	I Was Just Doing My Job	537	I'm In This To Go All The Way
517	I Will Remember That Day As Long As I Live	538	I'm Looking Forward To My Future Endeavors
518	I'd Love To See Him Play Another Year	539	I'm Looking Forward To The Challenge
519	I'd Say He's Done More Than That	540	I'm Not Going To Say Anything
520	If That Doesn't Bring Home A Gold Medal I Don't Know What Would	541	I'm Not Sure How He Pulled That Off
521	If We Chase Perfection We Can Catch Excellence	542	I'm Really Proud Of Our Guys
522	If Winning Isn't Everything Why Do They Keep Score	543	I'm Really Proud Of The Way Our Guys Hung In There
523	If You Can Accept Losing You Can't Win	544	I'm Speechless
524	If You Can't Imitate Him, Don't Copy Him	545	I'm Surprised He Fell This Far
525	If You Come To A Fork In The Road, Take It	546	I'm The Last One To Make Excuses
526	If You Don't Know Where You're Going Because You Might Not Get There	547	In Any Other Ballpark That's A Homerun
		548	In The Annals Of Sports
527	If You Don't Know Where You Are Going, You Will Wind Up Somewhere Else	549	In The Playoffs Anything Can Happen
		550	In The World Of Sports
528	If You Lose, You Go Home	551	Inspirational Play
529	If You Wrote The Script You Wouldn't Believe It	552	It Ain't Over 'Til The Fat Lady Sings
530	I'll Let The Racket Do The Talking	553	It Ain't The Heat It's The Humility
531	I'll Never Know Why They Traded Him	554	It All Depends On Where They Spot The Ball
		555	It Came Down To One

17

	Game
556	It Doesn't Matter Who They Play In The Next Round
557	It Feels Great To Be World Champions
558	It Gets Late Early Out There
559	It Hasn't Sunk In Yet
560	It Just Wasn't Meant To Be
561	It Looks Like They're Running Up The Score
562	It Means A Lot To The Fans
563	It Was A Hard-Fought Contest
564	It Was A Total Team Effort
565	It Was A Workman-Like Effort
566	It Was Door-To-Door Out There
567	It Wasn't Pretty But We'll Take It
568	It's A Guessing Game
569	It's Crunch Time
570	It's Gonna Be A War Out There
571	It's Gut-Check Time
572	It's Impossible To Get In A Conversation
573	It's A Beautiful Day For Baseball
574	It's A Game Of Field Position
575	It's A Low Line-Drive
576	It's A Nail Biter
577	It's A Nip And Tuck Game
578	It's A Real Pressure Cooker
579	It's A Rebuilding Year
580	It's A See-Saw Game
581	It's A Shame Somebody Has To Lose This Game
582	It's A Two Possession Game
583	It's A Whole New Ballgame

584	It's All About Speed
585	It's All About The Love Of The Game
586	It's All About Winning And Losing
587	It's Been A Crazy Ride
588	It's Been A Game Of Runs
589	It's Been A Great Ride
590	It's Been A Tale Of Two Halves
591	It's Been All Denver To This Point
592	It's Crunch Time
593	It's Decision Time
594	It's Do Or Die
595	It's Easy To Be A Monday Morning Quarterback
596	It's Going Down To The Wire
597	It's Going To Be A Battle Of Epic Proportions
598	It's Going To Be A Battle Of The Titans
599	It's Going To Be A Long Plane Ride Home
600	It's In The Record Book Now
601	It's Just Him Being Himself
602	It's Like Trying To Pin Down A Kangaroo On A Trampoline
603	It's Like Watching A Genius At Work
604	It's Never Happened In The World Series Competition
605	It's Never Happened In The World Series Competition And It Still Hasn't
606	It's Not Always About Speed
607	It's Not How You Start It's How You Finish

608	It's Not Whether You Get Knocked Down It's Whether You Get Up	630	Let's See If He Can Orchestrate A Comeback
609	It's Only A Matter Of Time Until He's Enshrined In The Hall-Of-Fame	631	Let's Take A Look At The Stats
		632	Lift Your Game
610	It's Raining Threes	633	Living In The Moment
611	It's The Grand-Daddy Of Them All	634	Look What I Found
612	It's The Nature Of This Business	635	Looks Like They're Content To Sit On The Lead
613	It's The World Series	636	Looks Like We'll Have Another Team Fall From The Ranks Of The Unbeaten
614	It's Theirs To Lose		
615	It's Time To Move On		
616	It's Time To Start Working On The Golf Game	637	Looks Like We've Got A Player Shaken Up
617	It's Tough To Win In A Hostile Environment	638	Looks Like We've Got Some Extra-Curricular Activity On The Field
618	Joe Is Going To Try And Settle Him Down	639	Major Player
619	Just Not Up To Par	640	Making That Look So Easy
620	Just Watching Him Is Worth The Price Of Admission	641	March Madness
		642	Mistakes Were Made
		643	Monday Morning Quarterbacking
621	Keep The Winning Streak Going	644	My Comments Were Taken Out Of Context
622	Keeping The Head Still Is Golf's One Universal Unarguable Fundamental	645	My Favorite Shots Are The Practice Swing And The Conceded Putt The Rest Cannot Be Mastered
623	Keeping Their Playoff Hopes Alive		
624	Kick Ass	646	My Hat's Off To Them
625	Kiss That One Goodbye - It's Outta Here	647	Never Do Card Tricks For The Group You Play Poker With
626	Last Week Was His Coming-Out Party		
		648	Never Give Up On The Ball
627	Leaders Aren't Born They Are Made	649	Never Stop Playing
628	Let The Celebration Begin	650	Never Take Your Eyes Off The Ball
629	Let's Go Back To The Clubhouse	651	Never Up, Never In
		652	No Lead Is Safe
		653	No Need To Panic, There's Plenty Of Time Left

19

654	No One's Talking Super Bowl Yet
655	Nobody Asked How You Looked, Just What You Shot
656	Nobody Goes There Anymore It's Too Crowded
657	Nobody Laid A Glove On Him
658	Not To Take Away Anything From Him
659	Nothing But Net
660	Now That Was Worthy Of A Gold Medal Performance
661	Now That's A Storybook Ending
662	Now That's Something To Smile About
663	Now There's A Superstar In The Making
664	Now There's A True Olympic Champion
665	Now They've Got Some Room To Operate
666	Now We've Got A Football Game
667	Now's The Time To Run Some Clock
668	Obviously I'm Disappointed Things Didn't Work Out
669	Off The Record
670	On Any Given Day Any Team Is Capable Of Beating Another Team
671	Once You Learn To Quit It Becomes A Habit
672	One Leg Take Down
673	One More For The Record Book
674	One Of The Most Exciting Games I've Ever Seen

675	One Of The Top Plays In Sports History
676	Only Perfect Practice Makes Perfect
677	Our Defense Didn't Show Up Today
678	Our Defense Was A Non-Factor
679	Our Fans Were The 12th Man Today
680	Out For Blood
681	Over-Exuberance Affected Our Better Judgment
682	Pennant Winning Victory
683	Perhaps The Best In The Game
684	Pete Is A Class Act
685	Pinch Hit
686	Placing First Is Not The Same As Winning
687	Play Ball
688	Players Like That Don't Come Around Very Often
689	Players Win Games Teams Win Championships
690	Playing Hardball
691	Playing In The World Series
692	Pop Those Champaign Corks
693	Post Season Rally
694	Pound For Pound He's The Best Fighter In The World
695	Practice Puts Brains In Your Muscles
696	Records Are Made To Be Broken
697	Ree-Jected
698	Right From The Horses Mouth
699	Score A Winner Every Time
700	Shattering The Recordbook
701	She Really Stuck The

	Landing
702	She Sacrificed So Much To Pursue Her Dreams Of Olympic Gold
703	She's The Favorite To Bring Home The Gold
704	She's The Sweetheart Of These Olympics
705	Show Me A Good Loser And I'll Show You A Loser
706	Slump? I Ain't In No Slump I Just Ain't Hitting
707	Something's Got To Give
708	Sports Central
709	Sports Do Not Build Character They Reveal It
710	Sportsman Of The Year
711	Squeeze Play
712	Statistics Can Be Misleading
713	Statistics Tell The Whole Story
714	Stepping Away From The Game
715	Stick A Fork In Him – He's Done
716	Sultan Of Swat
717	Surprise Me
718	Swing And A Miss
719	Ten Seconds Is Like An Eternity
720	Thanks, You Don't Look So Hot Yourself
721	That Ball Should Be Playable
722	That Came At An Inopportune Time
723	That Car Must Be Running On Fumes
724	That Changed The Complexion Of The Game

725	That Could Be The Knock-Out Punch
726	That Could Turn The Tide Of The Game
727	That Front Line Is 1000 Pounds Of Beef
728	That Goes Down In Sports History
729	That Hit Really Cleaned His Clock
730	That Keeps The Drive Alive
731	That Kick Splits The Uprights
732	That Lifted Their Spirits
733	That Looked Like A Blown Coverage
734	That Looked Like A Missed Assignment
735	That Looked Like A Simple Miscommunication
736	That Missed Extra Point Could Come Back To Haunt Them
737	That Old Arm Just Isn't What It Used To Be
738	That One Is Going To Hurt
739	That One's Going, Going - Gone
740	That Pass Looked Like A Wounded Duck
741	That Pass Was Right On The Money
742	That Pass Was Very Catchable
743	That Play Electrified The Crowd
744	That Puts You In The Game
745	That Really Helped His Cause
746	That Really Silenced The Crowd

747	That Really Took The Wind Out Of Their Sails	769	That Was A Page Right Out Of The Best Playbook I've Seen Lately
748	That Rookie Was In The Third Grade When He Started His Career	770	That Was A Pinpoint Pass
749	That Rookie Was In The Third Grade When His Started His Career	771	That Was A Real Heads-Up Play
		772	That Was A Shoestring Tackle
750	That Score Gives Them A Big Cushion	773	That Was A Smart Foul
751	That Score Makes It Respectable	774	That Was A Textbook Play
		775	That Was A Ticky-Tack Call
752	That Score Sealed The Victory	776	That Was A Timing Pattern
753	That Sealed Their Fate	777	That Was An Ill-Advised Pass
754	That Set The Tone Of The Game	778	That Was Just Huge
		779	That Was The Back Breaker
755	That Shattered The World Record	780	That Was The Big Play That Capped The Rally
756	That Shot Barely Drew Iron	781	That Was The Game's Defining Play
757	That Took The Crowd Out Of The Game	782	That Will Be A Hard Act To Follow
758	That Was A Challenge They Just Weren't Up To Today	783	That Will Be A Play That Goes Down Into The History Books
759	That Was A Circus Catch	784	That Will Be One Record That Will Never Be Broken
760	That Was A Game For The Record Books	785	That Will Make The Top 10 Plays Of All Times
761	That Was A Game Saving Tackle	786	That's Lights Out
762	That Was A Goal-Scorer's Goal	787	That'll Give Any Coach More Grey Hairs
763	That Was A Good Piece Of Hitting	788	That'll Give Me Even More Grey Hairs Just Watching
764	That Was A Good Piece Of Officiating	789	That'll Put Him On The National Scene
765	That Was A Gutsy Play	790	That's 14 Unanswered Points
766	That Was A Missed Opportunity	791	That's A Costly Turnover
767	That Was A Monster Drive	792	That's A Nail In The Coffin
768	That Was A Page Right Out Of Their Playbook	793	That's A Very Makeable Putt

794	That's Going To Be One Of Those Memorable Moments
795	That's Gotta Hurt
796	That's His Patented Jumper
797	That's How Legends Are Made
798	That's Just A Part Of Racing
799	That's Perhaps The Greatest Athlete Achievement I've Ever Witnessed
800	That's Stuff For The Highlight Film
801	That's The Key Statistic
802	That's The Key To The Game
803	That's The Kind Of Record You Don't Want To Break
804	That's The Old Ballgame
805	That's Too Little, Too Late
806	That's Unfortunate And Probably A Career Ending Injury
807	The Altitude Factor
808	The Ball Had Eyes
809	The Ball Just Didn't Bounce Our Way
810	The Ball Takes A Bizarre Bounce
811	The Ball Takes A Denver Bounce
812	The Ball Took A Bad Hop
813	The Ball Went Off The Side Of His Foot
814	The Best Offense Against The League's Best Defense
815	The Best Starting Season This Team Has Ever Had
816	The Best Team Won Today
817	The Big Game
818	The Big Guy Is Really Sweeping The Glass
819	The Big Leagues
820	The Biggest Stars In The Game
821	The Blackhawks Make A Wholesale Change
822	The Blitz Is Really Working
823	The Bodies Are Flying
824	The Best Team Left Their Finest Game On The Field
825	The Best Team Must Now Pin Their Hopes On His
826	The Car Got Up Into The Marbles
827	The Car Is All Tore Up
828	The Car's Pushing A Bit
829	The Car's Running A Little Loose
830	The Car's Running A Little Tight
831	The City Has Rallied Around This Team
832	The Clock Factor
833	The Clock Is Their Ally
834	The Clock Is Their Enemy
835	The Coach Has Been Under Fire
836	The Coach Is On The Hot Seat
837	The Coach's Head Is On The Chopping Block
838	The Competitive Juices Are Flowing
839	The Crowd Factor Is Really Kicking In
840	The Crowd Is Going Wild
841	The Crowd Is Really Into It Now
842	The Defense Had That Play Sniffed Out

23

843	The Defense Is Showing Blitz
844	The Defense Must Make A Stand
845	The Defensive Line Is Quick Off The Ball
846	The Desire To Win Clouded Our Judgment
847	The Experience Factor
848	The Fans Are Getting Their Money's Worth
849	The Fans Are On Their Feet
850	The Fans Really Got Their Money's Worth
851	The Fans Still Love Him
852	The Fatigue Factor
853	The Field Is A Frozen Tundra
854	The Final Four
855	The Final Score Is The Only Statistic That Matters
856	The Final Score Was Not A True Indication
857	The Final Series Of The Year
858	The Free Throw Shooting Has Been Anemic
859	The Game Has Passed Him By
860	The Game Is Everything
861	The Game Was A Lot Closer Than The Final Score Indicates
862	The Goalposts Are A Goalie's Best Friends
863	The Golden Age Of Baseball
864	The Guys In The Pits Won This One For Us
865	The Harder I Practice The Luckier I Get
866	The Heart Of The Game

867	The Humidity Factor
868	The Important Thing Is That We Won
869	The Injury Factor
870	The Intangibles Will Be The Key
871	The Irish Should Just Play Notre Dame Football
872	The Measure Of Who We Are Is What We Do With What We Have
873	The Meek May Inherit The Earth, But They'll Never Reach The Par 5 Green In 2
874	The Mental Factor
875	The Miracle Was Just Answered
876	The More I Practice, The Luckier I Get
877	The Most Colorful Athlete I've Ever Met
878	The Most Valuable Player In The League
879	The Motivation Factor
880	The New Coach Faces The Media For The First Time:
881	The Odds Of Failure Is Astronomical
882	The Officials Could Call Holding On Every Play
883	The Officials Were Right On Top Of That
884	The Only Place Success Comes Before Work Is In The Dictionary
885	The Only Way He'll Leave The Game Is If He's Carried Out On A Slate
886	The Other Teams Could Make Trouble For Us If They Win

887	The Pause Between The Action
888	The Perfect Strike When You Needed It
889	The Players Have Bought Into The System
890	The Prevent Defense Prevents You From Winning
891	The Psychological Factor
892	The Refs Should Let Them Play
893	The Revenge Factor
894	The Road To The Super Bowl Goes Through Green Bay
895	The Road To The Super Bowl Goes Through Miami
896	The Roof Just Caved In
897	The Rout Is On
898	The Scoreboard Doesn't Reflect The
899	The Season Is A Marathon - Not A Sprint
900	The Sports Greatest Stars
901	The Team Is Really High On Him
902	The Team Looks To Him For Leadership
903	The Team Made A Wholesale Change
904	The Team Really Covets This Guy
905	The Time Factor
906	The Towels Were So Thick There I Could Hardly Close My Suitcase
907	The Two Will Be Linked Forever
908	The Tying Run Is 90 Feet Away
909	The Tying Run Is At The

	Plate
910	The Wheels Just Fell Off
911	The Wild Card
912	The Wildcard Race Is Heating Up
913	The Wind Factor
914	The Wires Were Burning Hot
915	The Worst Day Of Fishing Beats The Best Day Of Working
916	The X-Factor
917	Their Backs Are Against The Wall
918	Their Defense Has Been Much Maligned
919	Their Defense Is Getting Shredded
920	Their Defense Is Starting To Assert Itself
921	Their Defense Is Tough In The Red Zone
922	Their Locker Room Must Look Like A MASH Unit
923	Their Magic Number Is Five
924	Their Offense Has Been Sputtering
925	Their Play Is Very Tentative
926	Their Secondary Looks Porous
927	Then It's The Axed Coach's Turn
928	There Are No Easy Games In This League
929	There Is No Such Thing As 'Natural Touch' Touch Is Something You Create By Hitting Millions Of Golf Balls
930	There Was A Lapse In Judgment

25

931	There Was An Error In Judgment	954	These Guys Never Doubted Themselves
932	There Were Too Many Defensive Lapses	955	These Opportunities Don't Happen Very Often
933	There Will Be Another Press Conference Where	956	These Two Teams Are Fighting Tooth And Nail
934	There's No "I" In Team	957	These Two Teams Are Going At It Like A Couple Of Heavyweights
935	There's No Question About It		
936	There's A Buck-30 Left In Regulation	958	These Two Teams Are Going To Slug It Out Till The Very Last Second
937	There's A Four-Base Blast		
938	There's A Lid On The Basket	959	These Two Teams Don't Like Each Other
939	There's A Log-Jam Atop The Leader Board	960	They Appear To Lack Consistency
940	There's A Quarterback Controversy On This Team	961	They Are Headed To The Post Season
941	There's Always Next Season	962	They Are One Strike Away
942	There's Bad Blood Between These Two Teams	963	They Ate Our Lunch
		964	They Can Go The Distance
943	There's Been A Lot Of Trash Talking	965	They Can Ill-Afford To Lose Him
944	There's God Then There's The Referee	966	They Can Put Up Big Numbers
945	There's No Love Lost Between These Two Teams	967	They Can Really Light Up The Scoreboard
946	There's No Tomorrow	968	They Can Score From Anywhere On The Ice
947	There's The Dagger		
948	There's The Insurance Run	969	They Can Smell Blood In The Water
949	These Fans Deserve A Winner	970	They Can Still Try The "Hail Mary"
950	These Guys Are Going Mano A Mano	971	They Can't Quite Put Them Away
951	These Guys Have Been Busting Their Butts	972	They Can't Afford To Get Lackadaisical
952	These Guys Have Been Working Their Tails Off	973	They Can't Be Intimidated
		974	They Can't Buy A Basket
953	These Guys Have Nothing To Be Ashamed Of	975	They Can't Cough It Up Here

976	They Can't Expect To Shut His Down Completely	998	They Had A Six Run Outburst In The Eighth Inning
977	They Can't Find Their Range	999	They Have A Few Choice Words For Each Other
978	They Can't Get Their Shots To Fall	1000	They Have A High-Octane Offense
979	They Can't Let The Crowd Faze Them	1001	They Have A Lot Of Big Game Experience
980	They Can't Look Past These Guys	1002	They Have A Lot Of Weapons
981	They Can't Stop The Clock So He'll Just Take A Knee	1003	They Have A Potent Offense
982	They Can't Take These Guys Lightly	1004	They Have A Stingy Defense
983	They Caught Us On An Off Night	1005	They Have A Strong Supporting Cast
984	They Control Their Own Destiny	1006	They Have A Swarming Defense
985	They Count On Him Week In And Week Out	1007	They Have A Tough Road To Hoe
986	They Diagrammed That Perfectly	1008	They Have Dangerous Deep Threats
987	They Do A Great Job Defensively	1009	They Have To Avoid A Big Letdown
988	They Dodged The Bullet There	1010	They Have To Believe In Themselves
989	They Don't Have Their Heads In The Game	1011	They Have To Bend But Not Break
990	They Feed Off Everyone's Energy	1012	They Have To Block Out Better
991	They Flushed His From The Pocket	1013	They Have To Body-Up On The Big Guy
992	They Gave It Their Best Shot	1014	They Have To Circle The Wagons
993	They Gave Us A Big Scare	1015	They Have To Come Out Of The Locker Room Fired Up
994	They Give You So Many Different Looks	1016	They Have To Come Together As A Team
995	They Got A Big Break There	1017	They Have To Crank It Up
996	They Got To Him Early	1018	They Have To Dictate The Tempo
997	They Got To Him Early And Often		

27

1019	They Have To Dig Deep	1039	They Have To Play Within Themselves
1020	They Have To Do The Things They've Been Doing All Season	1040	They Have To Pound It Out On The Ground
1021	They Have To Eliminate The Mental Mistakes	1041	They Have To Pound The Ball Inside
1022	They Have To Establish Their Running Game	1042	They Have To Pull Out All The Stops
1023	They Have To Find A Way To Put The Puck In The Net	1043	They Have To Remember What Got Them Here
1024	They Have To Find An Answer	1044	They Have To Rise To The Occasion
1025	They Have To Generate Some Offense	1045	They Have To Run The Table
1026	They Have To Get After It	1046	They Have To Shore Up Their Defense
1027	They Have To Get Back Into Their Offensive Rhythm	1047	They Have To Slowly Chip Away At This Lead
1028	They Have To Get Back On Track	1048	They Have To Stay Focused
1029	They Have To Get The Big Guy Involved In The Offense	1049	They Have To Stay Hungry
1030	They Have To Go Out And Take Care Of Business	1050	They Have To Step Up And Make Plays
1031	They Have To Keep The Continuity	1051	They Have To Step Up Their Offensive Production
1032	They Have To Leave Everything On The Field	1052	They Have To Step Up Their Run Production
1033	They Have To Make Plays On Both Sides Of The Ball	1053	They Have To Stick To Their Bread-And-Butter Offense
1034	They Have To Manufacture Some Runs	1054	They Have To Stick To Their Game Plan
1035	They Have To Open Up The Passing Lanes	1055	They Have To Stop The Big Play
1036	They Have To Play Ball-Control Offense	1056	They Have To Stop The Dribble Penetration
1037	They Have To Play Like They're Capable Of Playing	1057	They Have To Stretch Their Defense
1038	They Have To Play With Their Ears Pinned Back	1058	They Have To Suck It Up
		1059	They Have To Take Advantage Of Their Opportunities

28

1060	They Have To Take Care Of The Football	1082	They Need To Dominate The Offense
1061	They Have To Treat This Just Like Any Other Game	1083	They Need To Dominate The Offensive Glass
1062	They Have To Turn It Up A Notch	1084	They Need To Dominate The Paint
1063	They Have To Win Out	1085	They Need To Get A Win In Their Building
1064	They Just Made The Big Plays And We Didn't	1086	They Need To Get Healthy
1065	They Live And Die By Their Outside Shot	1087	They Need To Step Up To The Next Level
1066	They Look Out Of Synch	1088	They Need To Turn Up The Intensity
1067	They Managed To Back Into The Playoffs	1089	They Never Gave Up
1068	They Match Up Well	1090	They Out-Coached Us
1069	They Match-Up Well Size-Wise	1091	They Out-Hustled Us
		1092	They Out-Muscled Us
1070	They May Have Just Met Their Waterloo	1093	They Outplayed Us In Every Facet Of The Game
1071	They Move Well Without The Ball	1094	They Outplayed Us In Every Phase Of The Game
1072	They Must Capitalize On Their Opportunities	1095	They Own Us
1073	They Must Control The Tempo Of The Game	1096	They Pay Him To Make Those Catches
1074	They Must Maintain Their Composure	1097	They Play Above The Rim
1075	They Need A Defensive Stop	1098	They Play An Exciting Brand Of Basketball
1076	They Need A Timeout To Stop The Bleeding	1099	They Play An Up-Tempo Game
1077	They Need A Win To Stave Off Elimination	1100	They Play In-Your-Face Defense
1078	They Need A Win To Stop Their Five Game Skid	1101	They Play Punishing Defense
1079	They Need To Air It Out More	1102	They Play Tenacious Defense
		1103	They Play Tough "D"
1080	They Need To Dominate The Boards	1104	They Played Tough Defense Today
1081	They Need To Dominate The Line Of Scrimmage	1105	They Play Tremendous Pressure Defense
		1106	They Pride Themselves On Their Defense

29

1107	They Ran Into A Buzz Saw
1108	They Really Covet This Guy
1109	They Really Have To Take It To Them
1110	They Really Laid Him Out On That Hit
1111	They Score A Lot Of Points In Transition
1112	They Should Go Out There And Play Smash-Mouth Football
1113	They Should Just Go Out And Execute
1114	They Should Just Go Out There And Have Fun
1115	They Should Stick To The Fundamentals
1116	They Should Throw Their Game Plan Out The Window
1117	They Stepped Up And Made The Plays
1118	They Strike Fear In The Hearts Of Their Opponents
1119	They Wanted It More Than We Did
1120	They Went 80 Yards In The Ensuing Possession
1121	They Won't Be Denied
1122	They Won't Go Quietly
1123	They're A Better Team Than Their Record Indicates
1124	They're Blowing-Out The Other Team
1125	They're Down But Not Out
1126	They're Off To The Races Now
1127	They're Over-Achievers
1128	They've Been On A Roll
1129	They've Come Out Of Nowhere

1130	They've Pinned Their Hopes On This Young Guy
1131	They've Returned From Oblivion
1132	They'll Be Dancing In March
1133	They'll Have A Lot To Discuss At Halftime
1134	They'll Have To Find A Way To Contain Him
1135	They'll Have To Find A Way To Contain The Quarterback To Win This
1136	They'll Have To Find A Way To Limit What He Can Do
1137	They'll Have To Find A Way To Limit What His Can Do
1138	They'll Have To Settle For Three
1139	They're A Bit Banged Up
1140	They're A Blue Collar Team
1141	They're A Class Act
1142	They're A Dark Horse Team
1143	They're A Multi-Faceted Team
1144	They're A Real Cinderella Story
1145	They're A Team Of Destiny
1146	They're A Team To Be Reckoned With
1147	They're An Offensive-Minded Team
1148	They're Back On Their Heels
1149	They're Behind The Eight Ball
1150	They're Blowing The Game Wide Open
1151	They're Buzzing Around The Net
1152	They're Capable Of Making A Deep Run In The Post-Season

30

1153	They're Coming Off A Heartbreaking Loss	1173	They're In A Must-Win Situation
1154	They're Doing All The Little Things You Need To Win	1174	They're In Four Down Territory
1155	They're Drafting To Fill A Need	1175	They're In No Hurry At All
1156	They're Feeling Each Other Out	1176	They're In The Driver's Seat
1157	They're Fighty To Keep Their Hopes Alive	1177	They're In The Hurry-Up Offense
1158	They're Finally Getting The Respect They Deserve	1178	They're Just A Few Plays Away From Having A Perfect Season
1159	They're Finally Hitting Their Stride	1179	They're Just Exchanging Pleasantries
1160	They're Forced To Burn A Timeout	1180	They're Knocking On The Door
1161	They're Getting An Old-Fashioned Woodshed Whippin'	1181	They're Loaded For Bear
		1182	They're Loaded This Year
1162	They're Getting Beaten To The Puck	1183	They're Locked In A Defensive Battle
1163	They're Getting Some Good, Open Looks	1184	They're Looking At Third Down And Forever
1164	They're Going For A Three-Peat	1185	They're Looking For The Great Equalizer
1165	They're Going For Back-To-Back Championships	1186	They're Looking For An Equalizer In The Upcoming Draft
1166	They're Going For The Jugular	1187	They're Making A Living Behind The 3-Point Arc
1167	They're Going To Call A Timeout To Ice The Kicker	1188	They're Making A Lot Of Un-Forced Errors
1168	They're Going To Have To Make Some Adjustments	1189	They're Marching Down The Field
1169	They're Going To Tee-Off On Him	1190	They're Marking It Just Shy Of The 40 Yard-Line
1170	They're Having A Dream Season	1191	They're Mucking It Up In The Corner
1171	They're Having A Storybook Season	1192	They're No Pushovers
		1193	They're Not Just Happy To Be Here
1172	They're Hitting On All Cylinders	1194	They're Not Out Of It Yet

31

1195	They're Not Playing To Win - They're Playing Not To Lose		1217	They're Shooting The Lights Out
1196	They're Not Playing To Win They're Playing Not To Lose		1218	They're Shooting Well From Downtown
1197	They're Nursing Some Nagging Injuries		1219	They're Still Hanging Around
1198	They're On A Mission		1220	They're Still In The Hunt For That Final Playoff Berth
1199	They're On The Bubble		1221	They're Still In The Mix
1200	They're On The Outside Looking In		1222	They're Still Missing A Few Pieces To The Puzzle
1201	They're On The Ropes		1223	They're Still Talking Football
1202	They're Peaking At The Right Time		1224	They're Still Very Much Alive
1203	They're Peppering The Goaltender		1225	They're The Best
1204	They're Playing For Pride		1226	They're The Hardest Working Line In Hockey
1205	They're Playing In The Shadow Of Their Own Goalposts		1227	They're The League Cellar Dwellers
1206	They're Playing Inspired Defense		1228	They're The League Doormats
1207	They're Playing The Role Of Spoilers		1229	They're The Sentimental Favorites
1208	They're Playing With A Sense Of Urgency		1230	They're The Winningest Team In League History
1209	They're Playing With A Short Field		1231	They're Tough Competitors
1210	They're Playing With Swagger		1232	They're Trying To Milk The Clock
1211	They're Putting On A Clinic		1233	They're Within Striking Distance Now
1212	They're Really Banging In There		1234	They've Added A New Wrinkle To Their Offense
1213	They're Really Banging In There		1235	They've Answered The Call
1214	They're Running It Right Up The Gut		1236	They've Battled Back From The Brink Of Elimination
1215	They're Running Roughshod Over Them		1237	They've Been Here Before
1216	They're Self-Destructing		1238	They've Been Ice-Cold
			1239	They've Been Mathematically Eliminated
			1240	They've Been On Fire

1241	They've Been Playing With Confidence	1263	They've Got To Go Back And Re-Group
1242	They've Been Red-Hot	1264	They've Got To Ignore The Off-Field Distractions
1243	They've Been Riddled With Injuries	1265	They've Got To Knock Down Their Free Throws
1244	They've Been Struggling Offensively	1266	They've Got To Punch It In Here
1245	They've Been Struggling Offensively	1267	They've Got To Take It To The Big House
1246	They've Been Throwing Up Bricks	1268	They've Got To Take It To The Hole
1247	They've Built An Insurmountable Lead	1269	They've Got To Take It To The Rack
1248	They've Exploded For Six Runs Here In The Eighth Inning	1270	They've Got Tremendous Mental Toughness
1249	They've Gone Into Their Defensive Shell	1271	They've Gotten Over The Hump
1250	They've Gone To A Youth Movement	1272	They've Had A Few Players Go Down With Injuries
1251	They've Gone To The Well Once Too Often	1273	They've Had A Great Run
1252	They've Got A Few Guys Who Are Nicked Up	1274	They've Had Our Number All Season
1253	They've Got A Lot Of Depth	1275	They've Played A Soft Schedule
1254	They've Got A Tremendous Ball Club	1276	They've Scratched And Clawed Their Way Back Into The Game
1255	They've Got A Tremendous Ballclub	1277	Think How The Hell Are You Gonna Think And Hit At The Same Time
1256	They've Got Die-Hard Fans	1278	This Could Be A Sleeper Team
1257	They've Got Great Team Chemistry	1279	This Could Be The Turning Point
1258	They've Got Numbers	1280	This Could Be Two
1259	They've Got Some Good, Quality Wins	1281	This Could Be Two In A Row
1260	They've Got Some Players Who Are Ding'd Up	1282	This Could Get Ugly
1261	They've Got The Numbers	1283	This Franchise Has A Great Winning Tradition
1262	They've Got Their Backs Against The Wall		

33

1284	This Franchise Has A Storied Past		1306	This Is An Unfortunate Incident
1285	This Game Had A Storybook Ending		1307	This Is Awesome
			1308	This Is For All The Marbles
1286	This Game Has Gone True To Form		1309	This Is Just A Walk In The Park For Them Now
1287	This Game Has Turned Into A Chess Match		1310	This Is Like De-Ja-Vu All Over Again
1288	This Game Has Turned Into A Free-Throw Shooting Contest		1311	This Is Shaping Up To Be A Real Pitchers Duel
1289	This Game Has Turned Into A Track Meet		1312	This Is The Greatest Feeling In The World
1290	This Game Is A Slugfest		1313	This Is Their Deepest Penetration
1291	This Game Is Being Won In The Trenches		1314	This Is Their Watershed Game
1292	This Game Is For The Bragging Rights		1315	This Is Turning Into A Real Laugher
1293	This Game Is Getting Out Of Hand		1316	This Is What It's All About
1294	This Has Been A Very Special Team All Year		1317	This Map Award Belongs To The Whole Team
1295	This Has Been His Breakout Season		1318	This MVP Award Belongs To The Whole Team
			1319	This One Could Be Trouble
1296	This Is A Bitter Pill To Swallow		1320	This One Will Be Coming Back
1297	This Is A Dream Come True		1321	This One's In The Bag
1298	This Is A Game For The Ages		1322	This Place Is Bedlam
			1323	This Place Is Pandemonium
1299	This Is A Great Sports Town		1324	This Should Be A Chip Shot For Him
1300	This Is A Pivotal Game For Them		1325	This Team Always Seems To Find A Way To Win
1301	This Is A Real Shellacking		1326	This Team Has A Chance To Do Something Special
1302	This Is A Train Wreck		
1303	This Is A Very Different Ballgame		1327	This Team Has Finally Gotten Off The Schneid
1304	This Is Always A Tough Place To Play		1328	This Team Has Finally Learned How To Win
1305	This Is An Offensive Shootout		1329	This Team Has Overcome A Lot Of Adversity

34

1330	This Team Has Raised The Bar
1331	This Team Has Served Notice
1332	This Team Has Turned The Corner
1333	This Team Is Like A Family
1334	This Team Is Not Going To Sneak Up On Anybody
1335	This Team Is Really Starting To Gel
1336	This Team Is Running Like A Well-Oiled Machine
1337	This Team Is Searching To Find Its Identity
1338	This Team Is Showing Flashes Of Brilliance
1339	This Team Is Starting To Make Some Noise
1340	This Team Shows A Lot Of Character
1341	This Team Shows A Lot Of Heart
1342	This Team Shows A Lot Of Poise
1343	This Team Shows A Lot Of Pride
1344	This Team Shows A Lot Of Resiliency
1345	This Team Takes On The Personality Of Their Coach
1346	This Team Travels Well
1347	This Trade Changes The Balance Of Power In The Eastern Conference
1348	This Trade Helps Both Ball Clubs
1349	This Was A Confidence Booster
1350	This Was A Good Win For Us
1351	This Win Is For All The

	Fans
1352	This Win Was No Fluke
1353	This Would Be A Good Time For A Rally
1354	Those Players Form Their Nucleus
1355	Thought That Record Would Stand Until It Was Broken
1356	Three Up Three Down
1357	Three Up, Three Down
1358	Time To Take Another Tack
1359	Today Was One Of Those Days
1360	Today Will Be A Special Day In The Record Books
1361	Top Of The Baseball World
1362	Top Of The Inner
1363	Touch 'Em All
1364	Touch 'Em All!
1365	Tour De Force
1366	Turning The Tide
1367	Turnovers Killed Us
1368	Turnovers Will Be The Key
1369	Unfortunately He Can't Play Forever
1370	Unfortunately There Are Days Like This
1371	Warm Up The Bus
1372	We Are The Champions
1373	We Are The Winners
1374	We Beat A Very Good Team Today
1375	We Beat Ourselves
1376	We Brought Our A-Game
1377	We Came Out Flat
1378	We Came To Play
1379	We Came Up A Little Short
1380	We Can Still Hold Our Heads High

35

1381	We Didn't Get The Big Breaks Today
1382	We Didn't Get The Job Done
1383	We Didn't Lose The Game We Just Ran Out Of Time
1384	We Didn't Maintain The Intensity For The Entire 60 Minutes
1385	We Didn't Match Their Intensity
1386	We Didn't Play Like We're Capable Of Playing
1387	We Don't Care About Moral Victories
1388	We Don't Know The Extent Of His Injuries
1389	We Don't Play These Games On Paper
1390	We Dug Ourselves A Deep Hole
1391	We Feed Off The Energy Of Our Fans
1392	We Feel Fortunate
1393	We Finally Got The Monkey Off Our Backs
1394	We Got A Wake-Up Call
1395	We Had Our Chances But We Let Them Slip Away
1396	We Hate To Speculate On The Injury
1397	We Have To Look Forward
1398	We Hope That Cooler Heads Prevail
1399	We Interrupt This Broadcast
1400	We Knew This Would Be No Cakewalk
1401	We Knew We Had To Defend Our Home Turf
1402	We Knew What We Had To Do And Went Out

	And Did It
1403	We Lost Our Focus
1404	We Made A Statement Here Today
1405	We Made Our Own Breaks
1406	We Managed To Eke Out A Win
1407	We Need A Change Of Direction
1408	We Need A Clean Slate
1409	We Need Someone Who Can Take Us To The Next Level
1410	We Only Have To Look In The Mirror
1411	We Played Our Hearts Out
1412	We Proved We're The Better Team
1413	We Really Took It To 'Em
1414	We Sent A Message Here Today
1415	We Shocked The World
1416	We Shot Ourselves In The Foot
1417	We Snatched Victory Out Of The Jaws Of Defeat
1418	We Took Them Out Of Their Game
1419	We Were Really On Our Game
1420	We Weren't Going To Just Lie Down
1421	We Weren't Going To Just Roll Over
1422	We Weren't Mentally Prepared
1423	We're Taking It One Game At A Time
1424	Welcome To The NFL
1425	We'll Be Talking About This For A Long Time

1426	Well Jim, That's The Best He Could Have Done From There
1427	We'll Just Have To Put This Loss Behind Us
1428	We'll Miss Him A lot
1429	We'll Use This Win As A Stepping Stone To The Next Level
1430	Well, I Just Jinxed Him
1431	Well, Stranger Things Have Happened
1432	We're Glad To Get Out Of Here In The W Column
1433	We're Glad To Get Out Of Here With A Win
1434	We're Going To Get Things Turned Around
1435	We're Going To Right The Ship
1436	We're Going To Savor This Victory
1437	We're Going To The Playoffs
1438	We're Going To The Super Bowl
1439	We're Going To The World Series
1440	We're Going To Use This Win As A Building Block
1441	We're Happy We Could Pull This One Out At The End
1442	We're In The Business Of Winning
1443	We're Not Going To Rest On Our Laurels
1444	We're Tickled To Death
1445	We've Got A Bench-Clearing Brawl
1446	We've Got A Good, Solid Foundation To Build On
1447	We've Got A Late Flag

1448	We've Got A Real Barn-Burner
1449	We've Got An Intriguing Matchup
1450	We've Got The Greatest Fans In The World
1451	We've Got The League's Best Offense Against The League's Best Defense
1452	We've Got The League's Best Offense Against The League's Best Defense -- Something's Got To Give
1453	We've Just Witness A True Master Of The Game
1454	We've Reached The Quarter Pole
1455	We've Still Got Plenty Of Football Left
1456	What A Beautiful Golf Shot
1457	What A Bullet
1458	What A Difference A Week Makes
1459	What A Game Plan That Turned Out To Be
1460	What A Game We've Witnessed
1461	What A Great Read
1462	What A Match Up
1463	What A Season
1464	What A Shame To Waste All Those Great Shots On The Practice Range
1465	What A Statesperson For The Game
1466	What A Storybook Ending
1467	What A Turnover
1468	What An Ambassador For The Game
1469	What An Impressive Career

37

1470	What An Incredible Performance
1471	What An Incredible Turnaround
1472	What Can I Say We Gave It Our All
1473	What Counts In Sports Isn't Victory But The Magnificence Of The Struggle
1474	What Has He Done For You Lately
1475	What Records Hasn't He Broken
1476	What We Do In Life Echoes In Eternity
1477	When I Step Onto The Court I Don't Have To Think About Anything
1478	When It Stops Being Fun, It's Time To Quit
1479	When These Two Teams Get Together You Can Throw Out Their Records
1480	When You Look Back On The Game He'll Be Remember
1481	When You Put The Puck On The Net, Good Things Are Going To Happen
1482	When You Put The Puck On The Net, Good Things Happen
1483	Where Did He Come From
1484	Who Will Be This Year's Top Draft Pick
1485	Who Will Be This Year's Top Player
1486	Who'd Ever Think This Record Would Have Been Broken

1487	Why Buy Good Luggage When You Only Use It When You Travel
1488	Winning Is Habit Unfortunately So Is Losing
1489	Worth It's Weight In Gold
1490	Wow What A Game Absolutely Incredible
1491	Yeah, But We're Making Great Time
1492	You Are Certain To Hear Something Like:
1493	You Better Cut The Pizza In Four Pieces Because I'm Not Hungry Enough To Eat Six
1494	You Can Always Defend Upon Him
1495	You Can Depend On A Rabbit's Foot But Remember It Didn't Work For The Rabbit
1496	You Can Feel The Electricity
1497	You Can Feel The Momentum Swinging
1498	You Can Feel This One Slipping Away
1499	You Can Observe A Lot Just By Watching
1500	You Can See The Frustration Starting To Set In
1501	You Can't Abuse The Tires
1502	You Can't Go Into A Shop And Buy A Good Game Of Golf
1503	You Can't Steal First Base
1504	You Can't Stop Him; You Can Only Hope To Contain Him
1505	You Can't Teach That

1506	You Could Have Driven A Truck Through That Hole	1520	You Really Want To Come Away With Some Points
1507	You Couldn't Have Written A Better Script	1521	You Really Want To Come Away With Some Points When You're This Close
1508	You Don't Want To Give Up A Soft Goal Here	1522	You Should Always Go To Other People's Funerals; Otherwise, They Won't Come To Yours
1509	You Don't Win The Race On The First Lap		
1510	You Draft The Best Available Player	1523	You Still Don't Know How To Spell My Name
1511	You Dream About This As A Kid	1524	You Take What The Defense Gives You
1512	You Drive For Show	1525	You Win As A Team, You Lose As A Team
1513	You Drive For Show – Putt For Dough	1526	You Win Some And Lose Some
1514	You Give 100 Percent In The 1st Half... And If That Isn't Enough In The 2nd Half You Give What's Left	1527	You Wonder How Much Punishment He Can Absorb
		1528	You've Got To Give Them A Lot Of Credit
1515	You Got To Be Willing To Play The Game If You Want To Win	1529	You'll Be Hearing A Lot From Him
1516	You Have To Respect Their Athleticism	1530	You're Looking At A Future Hall Of Famer
1517	You Have To Respect Their Physicality	1531	You've Got To Finish To Win
1518	You Have To Respect Their Quickness	1532	You've Got To Hand It To Them
1519	You Know That Score Won't Hold Up	1533	You've Got To Pitch The Pitch

39

CLICHÉ
POPULAR EXPRESSIONS

1534	1% Inspiration And 99% Perspiration	1556	A Brand New Day
		1557	A Bread Winner
1535	24 Hours A Day 7 Days A Week	1558	A Breath Of Fresh Air
		1559	A Bubble Shy Of Plumb
1536	24/7/365	1560	A Bull In A China Shop
1537	A Backhanded Compliment	1561	A Bum Steer
1538	A Bad Hair Day	1562	A Bum Wrap
1539	A Bad Seed	1563	A Bump In The Road
1540	A Barn Burner	1564	A Bump On A Log
1541	A Basket Case	1565	A Camel Is A Horse Designed By Committee
1542	A Bear Market		
1543	A Big Head	1566	A Can Of Corn
1544	A Big Heart	1567	A Can Of Worms
1545	A Big Howdy Do Dah	1568	A Case Of The Dancer Blaming The Stage
1546	A Big Mouth		
1547	A Big Wig	1569	A Cash Cow
1548	A Bird In A Gilded Cage	1570	A Cast Of Thousands
1549	A Bird In The Hand Is Worth Two In The Bush	1571	A Cat Has Nine Lives
		1572	A Chain Is Only As Strong As It's Weakest Link
1550	A Bird's Eye View		
1551	A Black Eye	1573	A Chance Like No Other
1552	A Blast From The Past	1574	A Chance Of A Lifetime
1553	A Bone Of Contention	1575	A Cheap Knock Off
1554	A Bone To Pick	1576	A Chip Off The Old Block
1555	A Brain Drain	1577	A Clean Bill Of Health

1578	A Closed Mouth Gathers No Feet	1607	A Few Sandwiches Short Of A Picnic
1579	A Cock And Bull Story	1608	A Figure Of Speech
1580	A Complete Arsenal	1609	A Fish Out Of Water
1581	A Complete Collection	1610	A Flash In The Pan
1582	A Complete Package	1611	A Fly In The Ointment
1583	A Cult Of Personality	1612	A Fly On The Wall
1584	A Dagger In The Heart	1613	A Fool And His Money Are Soon Parted
1585	A Date That Will Live In Infamy	1614	A Fresh Approach
1586	A Date With Destiny	1615	A Fresh Pair Of Legs Up His Sleeve
1587	A Day Late And A Dollar Short	1616	A Fresh Start
1588	A Diamond In The Rough	1617	A Friend In Need Is A Friend In Deed
1589	A Dime A Dozen	1618	A Friend In Need Is A Friend Indeed
1590	A Dog Is A Man's Best Friend	1619	A Frog In My Throat
1591	A Dog's Life	1620	A Gold Digger
1592	A Drowning Man With Catch At A Straw	1621	A Gold Mine Of Information
1593	A Face Like A Bag Of Spanners	1622	A Good Beginning Makes A Good Ending
1594	A Face Like A Bulldog Chewing On A Wasp	1623	A Good Day's Work
1595	A Face Like A Burst Couch	1624	A Good Friend Of Mine
1596	A Face Like A Dropped Meat Pie	1625	A Good Man Is Hard To Find
1597	A Face Only A Mother Could Love	1626	A Good Rule Of Thumb
1598	A Face That Would Scare A Dog Out Of A Butcher Shop	1627	A Great Addition
1599	A Faint Heart Never A True Love Knows	1628	A Great Place To Start
1600	A Family Affair	1629	A Hair Of The Dog That Bit You
1601	A Far Cry	1630	A Half Baked Idea
1602	A Fast Buck	1631	A Hard Days Night
1603	A Fate Worse Than Death	1632	A Hard Lesson To Stomach
1604	A Feather In His Cap	1633	A Hard Lesson To Swallow
1605	A Few Bricks Shy	1634	A Heart Breaker
1606	A Few Fries Short Of A Happy Meal	1635	A Heart Of Stone
		1636	A High Degree Of Success
		1637	A Horse Of A Different Color
		1638	A Horseshoe Up His Ass

41

1639	A House Divided Against Itself Cannot Stand
1640	A Jack Of All Trades And A Master Of None
1641	A Journey Of A Thousand Miles Begins With The First Step
1642	A Kings' Ransom
1643	A Knock Off
1644	A Knockout
1645	A Kodak Moment
1646	A Last Ditch Effort
1647	A Lasting Impression
1648	A Laugh A Minute
1649	A Leap Of Faith
1650	A Legend In His Own Mind
1651	A Leopard Doesn't Change Its Spots
1652	A Liar Should Have A Good Memory
1653	A Light At The End Of The Tunnel
1654	A Line In The Sand
1655	A Little Bird Told Me
1656	A Little Knowledge Is A Dangerous Thing
1657	A Little Of This A Little Of That
1658	A Little Of This Little Of That
1659	A Little Off Kilter
1660	A Little Unorthodox
1661	A Little Yeast Works Through The Whole Batch Of Dough
1662	A Long Shot
1663	A Long Story Made Short
1664	A Long Time Coming
1665	A Long Ways Away
1666	A Loose Cannon
1667	A Lot Of Empty Flattery
1668	A Man Can't Be In Two Places At Once
1669	A Man For All Seasons
1670	A Man For All Season's
1671	A Man Is Known By The Company He Keeps
1672	A Man Who Is His Own Lawyer Has A Fool For A Client
1673	A Man's Got To Do What A Man's Got To Do
1674	A Man's Home Is His Castle
1675	A Man's Word Is A Good As His Bond
1676	A Marked Man
1677	A Matter Of Fact
1678	A Merry Heart Make A Cheerful Countenance
1679	A Mexican Standoff
1680	A Mind Is A Terrible Thing To Waste
1681	A Mint Of Money
1682	A Miss Is As Good As A Mile
1683	A Mother's Work Is Never Done.
1684	A Mover And A Shaker
1685	A Must Read
1686	A Nail Biter
1687	A Necessary Evil
1688	A New Broom Sweeps Clean
1689	A New Doo
1690	A New Lease On Life
1691	A New Perspective
1692	A No Brainer
1693	A Novel Twist
1694	A One Night Stand
1695	A Pain In The Butt
1696	A Pat On The Back
1697	A Penny For Your Thoughts

42

1698	A Penny Saved Is A Penny Earned	1731	A Soft Answer Turns Away Wrath
1699	A Picture's Worth A Thousand Words	1732	A Solution Exists For Every Problem
1700	A Piece Of Cake	1733	A Spoon Full Of Sugar Helps The Medicine Go Down
1701	A Pink Elephant		
1702	A Plague On Both Your Houses	1734	A Stick In The Eye
		1735	A Stick In The Mud
1703	A Poll Parrot Thinks Well O' Itself	1736	A Stitch In Time Saves Nine
		1737	A Stone's Throw Away
1704	A Poor Man Is Fain O' Little	1738	A Sweet Deal
1705	A Pretty Penny	1739	A Taste Of His Own Medicine
1706	A Promise Is A Promise		
1707	A Quick Fix	1740	A Tempest In A Teapot
1708	A Quick Sneak Peak	1741	A Thing Of Beauty Is A Joy For Ever
1709	A Rags To Riches Story		
1710	A Real Eye Opener	1742	A Ticket To Ride
1711	A Real Gulley Washer	1743	A Tight Wad
1712	A Reason Why	1744	A Tongue Lashing
1713	A Red Letter Day	1745	A Touch Of Class
1714	A Rifle For An Arm	1746	A Tree Is Known By It's Fruit
1715	A Rising Tide Lifts All Boats		
		1747	A Trial Balloon To Send Up Or Float
1716	A Rising Tide Will Lift All Boats Without Holes		
		1748	A Trojan Horse
1717	A Rolling Stone Gathers No Moss	1749	A Wake Up Call
		1750	A Walled Garden
1718	A Rose By Any Other Name Would Smell As Sweet	1751	A Watched Pot Never Boils
		1752	A Wealth Of Information
1719	A Rose Is A Rose Is A Rose	1753	A Welcomed Breath Of Fresh Air
1720	A Run For Your Money		
1721	A Secret Weapon	1754	A Wet Blanket
1722	A Shoestring Budget	1755	A White Elephant
1723	A Short Attention Span	1756	A White Knuckle Ride
1724	A Shot In The Arm	1757	A Windfall
1725	A Shot In The Dark	1758	A Winning Combination
1726	A Shotgun Wedding	1759	A Witch Hunt
1727	A Shut Out	1760	A Wolf In Sheep's Clothing
1728	A Sign Of The Times	1761	A Woman's Place Is In The Home
1729	A Simple Twist Of Fate		
1730	A Smoking Gun		

43

1762	A Woman's Work Is Never Done		1794	Add Insult To Injury
1763	A Word To The Wise Is Sufficient		1795	Adolescence Is A Marketing Ploy
1764	A Worker Bee		1796	Adversity Makes Strange Bedfellows
1765	A World Of Hurt		1797	After All Tomorrow Is Another Day
1766	Abandon Ship		1798	After My Own Heart
1767	Ablaze With Light		1799	After The Storm Comes A Calm
1768	About Face		1800	After They Made Her They Broke The Mold
1769	Above And Beyond The Call Of Duty		1801	Against All Odds
1770	Above Board		1802	Age Before Beauty
1771	Absence Makes The Heart Grow Fonder		1803	Ah To Be Young And Foolish
1772	Absolute Power Corrupts		1804	Ain't That A Bitch
1773	Absolute Power Corrupts Absolutely		1805	Ain't That A Kick In The Butt
1774	Accent The Positive And Eliminate The Negative		1806	Ain't Too Shabby
1775	Accentuate The Positive		1807	Airing Dirty Laundry
1776	Accessories Included		1808	Airing Out The Dirty Laundry
1777	Accident Prone		1809	Albeit For All The Wrong Reasons
1778	According To Hoyle		1810	Alive And Kicking
1779	Ace In The Hole		1811	All At Once
1780	Ace Up His Sleeve		1812	All Balled Up In A Knot
1781	Ace Up Your Sleeve		1813	All Bent Out Of Shape
1782	Achilles Heel		1814	All Bets Are Off
1783	Acid Test		1815	All Dressed Up And Nowhere To Go
1784	Acorn Doesn't Fall Far From The Tree		1816	All Eyes/Ears
1785	Acquired Taste		1817	All Fired Up
1786	Across The Universe		1818	All For One And One For All
1787	Act Like A Gentleman		1819	All Ginned Up
1788	Act Like A Lady		1820	All Good Things Come In Threes
1789	Act Now While It's Fresh In Your Mind		1821	All Good Things Come To Those Who Wait
1790	Act Upon Your Intuition			
1791	Actions Form Habits			
1792	Actions Speak Louder Than Words			
1793	Adam's Apple			

44

1822	All Good Things Must Come To An End		1857	All The Kings Horses And All The Kings Men
1823	All Hands On Deck		1858	All The Way
1824	All Hands To The Pump		1859	All The World's A Stage
1825	All Hell Broke Loose		1860	All Things Are Possible
1826	All I Ever Need Is You		1861	All Things To All Men
1827	All I Have To Do Is Dream		1862	All Thumbs
1828	All In A Day's Work		1863	All Wet Behind The Ears
1829	All In Due Time		1864	All Work And No Play Makes Jack A Dull Boy
1830	All In Good Time			
1831	All In The Family		1865	All You Need Is Love
1832	All Is Not Gold That Glitters		1866	All Your Ducks In A Row
1833	All Is Vanity		1867	Alley Cat
1834	All Men Are Created Equal		1868	All's Fair In Love And War
1835	All Of A Sudden		1869	All's Well That Ends Well
1836	All Or Nothing		1870	Almost Home
1837	All Or Nothing At All		1871	Along For The Ride
1838	All Over But The Shouting		1872	Alpha And Omega
1839	All Over Me Like A Cheap Suit		1873	Already Got One Paw On The Chicken Coop
1840	All Over The Map		1874	Alrighty Then
1841	All Paled In Comparison		1875	Altitude Is Determined By Attitude
1842	All Quiet On The Home Front		1876	Always A Bridesmaid Never The Bride
1843	All Quiet On The Western Front		1877	Always In Stock
1844	All Right Now		1878	Always In Style
1845	All Roads Lead To Rome		1879	Always Look On The Bright Side
1846	All Shook Up			
1847	All Sixes And Sevens		1880	Always On Top
1848	All Summer Long		1881	Always Put Your Best Foot Forward
1849	All Systems Go		1882	Am I My Brother's Keeper
1850	All Talk And No Action		1883	Ambulance Chaser
1851	All That Glitters Is Not Gold		1884	An Abrupt Ending
1852	All That Jazz		1885	An Ace In The Hole
1853	All The Bells And Whistles		1886	An Albatross Around Your Neck
1854	All The Bells And Whistles You Could Ever Want			
1855	All The Bits And Pieces		1887	An American Dream
1856	All The Grizzly Details		1888	An Apple A Day Keeps The Doctor Away

45

1889	An Arm And A Leg
1890	An Army Of One
1891	An Axe To Grind
1892	An Earful
1893	An Elephant Never Forgets
1894	An Emotional Roller Coaster
1895	An Empty Sack Can Not Stand Upright
1896	An Eye For An Eye And A Tooth For A Tooth
1897	An Eye Opener
1898	An Idle Mind Is The Devil's Playground
1899	An Ill Fated Idea
1900	An Ill Wind That Blows No Good
1901	An Oldie But A Goodie
1902	An Open Book
1903	An Ounce Of Prevention Is Worth A Pound Of Cure
1904	An Overnight Success
1905	An Uphill Battle
1906	Anchors Away
1907	And Much Much More
1908	And Never The Twain Shall Meet
1909	And Now A Message From Our Sponsor
1910	And That Was That
1911	And That's Just Scratching The Surface
1912	And That's The Way It Is
1913	And That's The Way It Was
1914	And The Winner Is
1915	And We're Not Just Whistling Dixie
1916	And You Can Take That To The Bank
1917	Another Brick In The Wall
1918	Another Country

	Heard From
1919	Another Day Another Dollar
1920	Another Nail In The Coffin
1921	Another One Bites The Dust
1922	Ants In His Pants
1923	Anvil Chorus
1924	Any Day Now
1925	Any Dream Will Do
1926	Any Friend Of Yours Is A Friend Of Mine
1927	Any Port In A Storm
1928	Any Time Any Place
1929	Any Time Any Place Any Where
1930	Any Way You Want It
1931	Anyhoo
1932	Anything Goes
1933	Anything Is Possible
1934	Anything That Can Go Wrong
1935	Anything Worth Doing Is Worth Doing Well
1936	Anyway Back To The Story
1937	Appearances Are Deceiving
1938	Apple Doesn't Fall Far From The Tree
1939	Apple Of My Eye
1940	Apple Polishing
1941	April Showers Bring May Flowers
1942	Are We There Yet
1943	Are You A Good Flirt
1944	Are You A Man Or A Mouse
1945	Are You Fair Dinkum
1946	Are You Going To Be A Stick In The Mud
1947	Are You Lonesome Tonight
1948	Are You Stuck On Start
1949	Armed To The Teeth
1950	Around The Horn

1951	Art Is Long - It's Life That's Short
1952	As A Matter Of Fact
1953	As All Get Out
1954	As American As Apple Pie
1955	As Beautiful As The Day Is Long
1956	As Cute As A Buttons
1957	As Dense As A London Fog
1958	As Easy As Falling Off A Log
1959	As Far As The Eye Can See
1960	As Good As Gold
1961	As Good As It Gets
1962	As Honest As The Day Is Long
1963	As Horny As A Three Balled Tomcat
1964	As If I Care
1965	As Important As It Used To Be
1966	As Incredible As It Seems
1967	As Luck Would Have It
1968	As Old As The Hills
1969	As Plain As The Nose On Your Face
1970	As Scarce As Hen's Teeth
1971	As Simple As That
1972	As Snug As A Bug In A Rug
1973	As Sweet As American Pie
1974	As Tender As A Mother's Heart
1975	As The Crow Flies
1976	As The Twig Is Bent So Grows The Tree
1977	As The Wind Blows
1978	As Useful As A Lead Balloon
1979	As Useful As Tits On A Bull
1980	As Welcome As A Skunk At A Lawn Party
1981	As Ye Sow

	So Shall Ye Reap
1982	As You Wish
1983	Ashes To Ashes Dust To Dust
1984	Ask For More
1985	Ask Me No Questions And I'll Tell You No Lies
1986	Ask Not What Your Country Can Do For You But What You Can Do For Your Country
1987	Asleep At The Wheel
1988	Ass Backwards
1989	Ass Over Tea Kettle
1990	Ass Over The Tea Kettle
1991	At A Glance
1992	At Any Rate
1993	At Daggers Drawn
1994	At First Blush
1995	At First Glance
1996	At First Light
1997	At Logger Heads
1998	At Loose Ends
1999	At My Signal - Unleash Hell
2000	At The 11th Hour
2001	At The Crack Of Dawn
2002	At The Drop Of A Hat
2003	At The Eleventh Hour
2004	At The End Of My Rope
2005	At The End Of The Day
2006	At The End Of The Pecking Order
2007	At The Last Minute
2008	At The Top Of His Game
2009	At The Touch Of A Button
2010	At Wits' End
2011	At Your Fingertips
2012	At Your Request
2013	Atta Boy
2014	Atta Girl
2015	Auld Lang Syne

2016	Available Around The World
2017	Avoid A Quick Back Swing
2018	Avoid The Hassle
2019	Awake Counting Sheep
2020	Ax To Grind
2021	Babe In The Woods
2022	Baby Blues
2023	Baby Boomer
2024	Baby Kisser
2025	Baby One More Time
2026	Baby You're The Greatest
2027	Back Against The Wall
2028	Back And Fill
2029	Back Breaker
2030	Back From The Dead
2031	Back Handed Comment
2032	Back In A Sec
2033	Back In The Good Old Days
2034	Back In The Olden Days
2035	Back In The Saddle
2036	Back It Up
2037	Back Of The Seat Of The Envelope Calculation
2038	Back On My Feet Again
2039	Back On Your Feet
2040	Back Seat Driver
2041	Back Stabber
2042	Back Straight Knees Bent Feet An Shoulder Width Apart
2043	Back To Square One
2044	Back To The Drawing Board
2045	Back To The Salt Mines
2046	Backed Into A Corner
2047	Backhanded Compliment
2048	Bad Blood
2049	Bad Call
2050	Bad Egg
2051	Bad Hair Day
2052	Bad Money Drives Out

	Good
2053	Bad News Travels Fast
2054	Bad Penny Always Turns Up
2055	Bad Seed
2056	Bad To The Bone
2057	Bad Wrap
2058	Badda Bing
2059	Bag And Baggage
2060	Bags All Packed And Ready To Go
2061	Bait And Switch
2062	Baked And Shaked
2063	Baker's Dozen
2064	Balcony Is Closed
2065	Bald Faced Liar
2066	Balder Dash
2067	Ball Is In Your Court
2068	Balls Out
2069	Balls To The Wall
2070	Bally Hoo
2071	Baloney
2072	Bam Boozzle
2073	Bambino
2074	Banding Together To Beat The Odds
2075	Bang For The Buck
2076	Bang The Drum
2077	Banging Your Head Against A Brick Wall
2078	Bank On It
2079	Baptism By Fire
2080	Bare Bones
2081	Bare Face
2082	Barge Right In
2083	Barking Up The Wrong Tree
2084	Barn Burner
2085	Barn Storm
2086	Basket Case
2087	Bass Ackwards
2088	Bat An Eyelid

48

2089	Bat The Idea Around	2120	Beat It
2090	Bated Breath	2121	Beat On The Street
2091	Bats In The Belfry	2122	Beat Swords Into Ploughshares
2092	Batten Down The Hatches - Lower The Boom - Raise The Misenmast	2123	Beat The Band
		2124	Beat The Clock
2093	Battle Line Is Drawn	2125	Beat The Living Daylights Out Of You
2094	Battle Of The Bulge	2126	Beat The Rap
2095	Battling Windmills	2127	Beating A Dead Horse
2096	Be All Ears	2128	Beating Around The Bush
2097	Be All You Can Be	2129	Beating The Bushes
2098	Be Back Later	2130	Beats Me
2099	Be Back Soon	2131	Beautiful Loser
2100	Be Careful	2132	Beauty And The Beast
2101	Be Careful What You Wish For	2133	Beauty Is A Fading Flower
		2134	Beauty Is In The Eye Of The Beholder
2102	Be Careful You Might Get What You Wish For	2135	Beauty Is Only Skin Deep
2103	Be Consistent Or Be Inconsistent But Don't Vacillate	2136	Beauty Is Truth - Truth Is Beauty
		2137	Because You're Worth It
2104	Be In The Same Boat	2138	Beck And Call
2105	Be It Ever So Humble There's No Place Like Home	2139	Become A Fly On The Wall
		2140	Bed Of Roses
		2141	Bee In Her Bonnet
2106	Be My Sugar Daddy	2142	Been Down So Long
2107	Be Nice To The People On The Way Up	2143	Been There Done That
		2144	Been There Seen It Done That
2108	Be Right Back		
2109	Be Right Here	2145	Bee's Knees
2110	Be Swept Away	2146	Before I Explain
2111	Be The Ball	2147	Before They're Gone
2112	Be The Envy Of The Neighborhood	2148	Before You Go
		2149	Beggars Can't Be Choosers
2113	Be There Or Be Square	2150	Begs The Question
2114	Beach Comer	2151	Behind Every Great Man Is A Great Woman
2115	Beacon Of Hope		
2116	Beam Me Up Scotty	2152	Behind The Curtain
2117	Bears And Bulls	2153	Behind The Eight Ball
2118	Beat A Dead Horse	2154	Behind The Times
2119	Beat Around The Bush		

49

2155	Being In The Right Place At The Right Time	2186	Best Things Come In Small Packages
2156	Being Led Down The Garden Path	2187	Best Things In Life Are Free
2157	Being Naturally Right Footed He Doesn't Often Chance His Arm With His Left Foot	2188	Bet It All
		2189	Bet The Farm
		2190	Bet Your Bottom Dollar
2158	Believe In Yourself	2191	Better And Better
2159	Believe It Or Not	2192	Better Half
2160	Believe It's Possible	2193	Better Half The
2161	Believe Nothing You Hear And Half Of What You See	2194	Better Late Than Never
		2195	Better Light A Candle Than Curse The Darkness
2162	Bell The Cat	2196	Better Luck Next Time
2163	Belle Of The Ball	2197	Better Outlook On Life
2164	Belly Up To The Bar	2198	Better Safe Than Sorry
2165	Below The Belt	2199	Better Than A Kick In The Teeth
2166	Below The Fold		
2167	Bend Me Shape Me	2200	Better Than Anything
2168	Bend Over	2201	Better Than Ever
2169	Bend Over Backwards	2202	Better Than Expected
2170	Beside The Mark	2203	Better Than The Average Bear
2171	Besides Yourself		
2172	Best Deal Ever	2204	Better The Devil You Know Than The Devil You Don't
2173	Best Defense Is A Good Offense		
		2205	Better To Give Than Receive
2174	Best Foot Forward		
2175	Best In Show	2206	Better To Have Loved And Lost Than Never To Have Loved At All
2176	Best Is Yet To Come		
2177	Best Kept Secrets		
2178	Best Laid Plans Of Mice And Men	2207	Better To Light One Candle Than To Curse The Darkness
2179	Best Of Both Worlds		
2180	Best Of Breed	2208	Better To Remain Silent And Be Thought A Fool Than To Speak And Remove All Doubt
2181	Best Possible Timing		
2182	Best Seat In The House		
2183	Best Selling Author		
2184	Best Selling Price	2209	Betting The Farm
2185	Best Thing Since Sliced Bread	2210	Between A Rock And A Hard Place
		2211	Between The Devil And The Deep Blue Sea
		2212	Beware Of Imitators

2213	Beware The Anger Of A Patient Man
2214	Beware The Ides Of March
2215	Beyond Borders
2216	Beyond The Beam
2217	Beyond The Obvious
2218	Beyond The Pale
2219	Big As A House
2220	Big As Life
2221	Big Brother Is Watching
2222	Big Deal
2223	Big Girls Don't Cry
2224	Big Head
2225	Big Heart
2226	Big Mouth
2227	Big Picture
2228	Big Red Switch
2229	Big Stick
2230	Big Wig
2231	Bigger Is Better
2232	Bigger They Are The Harder They Fall
2233	Biggest And Brightest
2234	Biggest Fish In The Sea
2235	Biggest Little Lie
2236	Biggest Little Secret
2237	Biggest Toad In The Puddle
2238	Biological Clock Is Ticking
2239	Bird In A Gilded Cage
2240	Bird In The Hand Is Worth Two In The Bush
2241	Birds Of A Feather Flock Together
2242	Bite Me
2243	Bite Off More Than You Can Chew
2244	Bite The Bucket
2245	Bite The Bullet
2246	Bite The Dust
2247	Bite Your Lip
2248	Bite Your Tongue

2249	Bitter Pill To Swallow
2250	Black As Pitch
2251	Black Dog
2252	Black Eye
2253	Blame It On My Youth
2254	Blast From The Past
2255	Blaze A New Trail
2256	Blaze Of Glory
2257	Blazing New Trails
2258	Blazing The Path
2259	Blew Him Away
2260	Blew His Wad
2261	Blind As A Bat
2262	Blind Leading The Blind
2263	Blood Brothers
2264	Blood Is Thicker Than Water
2265	Blood Money
2266	Blood Sweat And Tears
2267	Blood Toil Tears And Sweat
2268	Bloody Mary
2269	Bloody Murder
2270	Bloom Is Off The Rose
2271	Bloom Where You're Planted
2272	Blow A Gasket
2273	Blow Chow
2274	Blow Chunks
2275	Blow It
2276	Blow Me Down
2277	Blow The Whistle
2278	Blow Your Brains Out
2279	Blow Your Own Horn
2280	Blowing Hot And Cold
2281	Blowing Smoke Up My Ass
2282	Blowing Your Top
2283	Blown Away
2284	Blows The Doors Off The Barn
2285	Blue Blooded
2286	Blue Collar Worker

2287	Blue In The Face	2325	Boy Howdy
2288	Blue Light Special	2326	Boys In The Hood
2289	Blue Monday	2327	Boys Will Be Boys
2290	Blue Moon	2328	Bragging Rights
2291	Blue Nose	2329	Brain Drain
2292	Blunt Words Have The Sharpest Edge	2330	Brain Dump
		2331	Brain Trust
2293	Bob Tail	2332	Brand Spanking New
2294	Body And Soul	2333	Bread Always Falls Butter Side Down
2295	Body Is Still Warm		
2296	Body Slam	2334	Bread And Butter
2297	Boffo	2335	Bread Winner
2298	Boiling Mad	2336	Break A Leg
2299	Bolt From The Blue	2337	Break It Down
2300	Bombed	2338	Break Ranks
2301	Bombs Away	2339	Break The Bank
2302	Bond James Bond	2340	Break The Ice
2303	Bone Chilling Cold	2341	Breaking Up Is Hard To Do
2304	Bone Of Contention	2342	Breathing Down My Neck
2305	Bone To Pick	2343	Brevity Is The Soul Of Wit
2306	Bone Up On	2344	Bridge Over Trouble Water
2307	Book Em Danno	2345	Bridging The Divide
2308	Book Of Love	2346	Bridging The Gap
2309	Bored To Tears	2347	Bright As A Button
2310	Born To Be Wild	2348	Bright Future
2311	Born With A Silver Spoon In His Mouth	2349	Brim Stone
		2350	Bring Down The House
2312	Both Barrels	2351	Bring It
2313	Both Feet Firmly Planted On The Ground	2352	Bring It On
		2353	Bring Out The Gimp
2314	Bottom Fell Out	2354	Bring Sand To The Beach
2315	Bottom Line	2355	Bring Something To The Table
2316	Bottom Out		
2317	Bottoms Up	2356	Bringing Home The Bacon
2318	Bought The Farm	2357	Broke The Bank
2319	Bounce Back	2358	Brother Can You Spare A Dime
2320	Bowl Someone Over		
2321	Box Of Birds	2359	Brown Nose
2322	Box Of Fluffy Ducks	2360	Brush Off
2323	Box Yourself In	2361	Bubble Shy Of Plumb
2324	Boxed In	2362	Buck A Roo

2363	Buck Naked
2364	Buck Rogers
2365	Buck Stops Here
2366	Buck The System
2367	Buckle Down
2368	Buckle Under
2369	Buddy Can You Spare A Dime
2370	Bug A Boo
2371	Build A Better Mousetrap And The World Will Beat A Path To Your Door
2372	Build Me Up Buttercup
2373	Built As A Memorial
2374	Built Like A Brick Shit House
2375	Built Like A Tank
2376	Built To Last
2377	Bull Session
2378	Bum Steer
2379	Bum Wrap
2380	Bummer
2381	Bump In The Road
2382	Bump On A Log
2383	Bun In The Oven
2384	Burn The Candle At Both Ends
2385	Burn The Midnight Oil
2386	Burn Your Bridges
2387	Burn Your Ships
2388	Burning Down The House
2389	Burning Rubber
2390	Burning The Midnight Oil
2391	Burning Up The Track
2392	Burst At The Seams
2393	Bury The Hatchet
2394	Bury Your Head In The Sand
2395	Busier Than A One-Armed Paper Hanger
2396	Business As Usual
2397	Business At Hand
2398	Business Before Pleasure
2399	Business Is Business
2400	Business May Bring Money But Friendship Hardly Ever Does
2401	Busman's Holiday
2402	Bust Your Balls
2403	Busted
2404	Busting A Gut
2405	Busting Your Chops
2406	Busy As A Bear In A Beehive
2407	Busy As A Beaver
2408	Busy As A Bee
2409	Busy As A Cat Trying To Bury Shit On A Hot Tin Roof
2410	Busy As A One-Legged Man In An Ass Kicking Contest
2411	Busy Hands Are Happy Hands
2412	But Enough About Me
2413	But Out
2414	But Then Again
2415	But There's More
2416	But They Will Never Take Our Freedom
2417	Butter Him Up
2418	Butter Wouldn't Melt In His Mouth
2419	Butter Your Bread On The Wrong Side
2420	Butterflies In His Stomach
2421	Buttlegging
2422	Buy Into
2423	Buy It For The Price Of A Skinny Chicken
2424	Buy Something For A Song
2425	Buy The Farm
2426	Buy The Numbers
2427	Buzz Saw

2428	By All Means After You
2429	By And Large
2430	By Hook Or By Crook
2431	By Jove
2432	By Special Arrangement
2433	By The Boatload
2434	By The Book
2435	By The Same Token
2436	By The Skin Of One's Teeth
2437	By The Truckload
2438	By The Way
2439	Caca Mimi Scheme
2440	California Dreamin'
2441	Call A Spade A Spade
2442	Call It A Day
2443	Call Me
2444	Call Me Irresponsible
2445	Call Me Ishmael
2446	Call Off The Dogs
2447	Call Someone On The Carpet
2448	Call The Shots
2449	Call The Turn
2450	Called On The Carpet
2451	Calling The Shots
2452	Calm Before The Storm
2453	Came To The Conclusion Of His Travelling Thoughts
2454	Can It
2455	Can Lead A Horse To Water But
2456	Can Of Corn
2457	Can Of Whoop Ass
2458	Can Of Worms
2459	Can't Beat That With A Stick
2460	Can't Blame Him For Trying
2461	Can't Cut It
2462	Can't Find His Way Out Of A Paper Bag

2463	Can't For The Life Of Me Remember
2464	Can't Get A Word In Edgewise
2465	Can't Get To First Base With Her
2466	Can't Have Your Cake And Eat It Too
2467	Can't Help Falling In Love
2468	Can't Hold A Candle
2469	Can't Hold A Candle To The Day
2470	Can't Hold A Feather
2471	Can't Hold Water
2472	Can't Learn To Swim Without Getting In The Water
2473	Can't Pull The Wool Over My Eyes
2474	Can't Say Enough About Him
2475	Can't Say I Would
2476	Can't Squeeze Blood Out Of A Turnip
2477	Can't Take My Eyes Off You
2478	Can't Teach An Old Dog New Tricks
2479	Can't Win For Losing
2480	Cantankerous
2481	Card Shark
2482	Carpe Diem - Seize The Day
2483	Carpet Bagger
2484	Carrot On A Stick
2485	Carry The Torch
2486	Carrying Coal To Newcastle
2487	Carte Blanche
2488	Carve Out A Niche
2489	Case In Point
2490	Case Of The Dancer Blaming The Stage
2491	Cash Cow
2492	Cash In

2493	Cash In Your Chips
2494	Cash Is King
2495	Cash It In
2496	Cash On Demand
2497	Cash On The Barrel
2498	Cash On The Barrelhead
2499	Cast A Very Long Shadow
2500	Cast Your Bread Upon The Waters
2501	Cat Got Your Tongue
2502	Cat Like Grace
2503	Cat Nap
2504	Cat On A Hot Tin Roof
2505	Catch 22
2506	Catch A Falling Knife
2507	Catch As Catch Can
2508	Catch Forty Winks
2509	Catch Hell If I Do Catch Hell If I Don't
2510	Catch My Drift
2511	Catch Of The Day
2512	Catch On
2513	Catching Some ZZZ's
2514	Cat's Meow
2515	Cat's Whiskers
2516	Caught Between A Rock And A Hard Place
2517	Caught In The Crossfire
2518	Caught Me Off Guard
2519	Caught Red Handed
2520	Caught With His Hands In The Till
2521	Caught With His Pants Down
2522	Caught With Your Hand In The Cookie Jar
2523	Cause And Effect
2524	Celebrate A Birthday Bash
2525	Center Of Attention
2526	Center Of Attraction
2527	C'est La Vie

2528	Chain Is Only As Strong As It's Weakest Link
2529	Champagne Tastes On A Beer Budget
2530	Change Is Constant
2531	Change Your Mind
2532	Change Your Tune
2533	Changing Hands
2534	Changing Times
2535	Changing Your Life For The Better
2536	Chapter And Verse
2537	Char Woman
2538	Character Fixes Our Destiny
2539	Charity Begins At Home
2540	Charlie Horse
2541	Chatty Cathy
2542	Cheap At Half The Price
2543	Cheap But Effective
2544	Cheap Date
2545	Cheap Shot
2546	Cheap Skate
2547	Cheap Trick
2548	Check Is In The Mail
2549	Check It Out
2550	Check's In The Mail
2551	Cheese Cake
2552	Cheesy Does It
2553	Cherchez la Femme
2554	Chew On
2555	Chew Out
2556	Chew The Fat
2557	Chew The Rag
2558	Chewing Nails And Spitting Tacks
2559	Chewing The Fat
2560	Chicken In Every Pot
2561	Chickens Have Come Home To Roost
2562	Chicks Rule

2563	Chief Cook And Bottle Washer	2597	Close Enough For Horseshoes And Hand Grenades
2564	Children Should Be Seen And Not Heard	2598	Close Enough For Rocket Science
2565	Childs Play	2599	Close Only Counts In Horseshoes
2566	Chill Out	2600	Close Ranks
2567	Chip In	2601	Close The Barn Door
2568	Chip Off The Old Block	2602	Closing The Barn Door After The Horse Has Bolted
2569	Chip On Your Shoulder	2603	Clothes Make The Man
2570	Chivalry Is Not Dead	2604	Clucking And Bucking With The Other Hens
2571	Chock Full Of Ideas	2605	Clue Me In
2572	Chomping At The Bit	2606	Cock And Bull Story
2573	Choose Wisely	2607	Code Blue
2574	Choose Your Partner Wisely	2608	Code Red
2575	Chopped Liver	2609	Coin A Phrase
2576	Chow Down	2610	Cold As A Witch's Tit
2577	Circle The Wagons	2611	Cold As Blue Blazes
2578	Clam Down	2612	Cold As Cucumber
2579	Clash Of The Titans	2613	Cold As Ice
2580	Clean Bill Of Health	2614	Cold Day In Hell
2581	Clean Sweep	2615	Cold Enough To Freeze The Balls Off A Brass Monkey
2582	Clean Up Fast	2616	Cold Feet
2583	Clean Your Clock	2617	Cold Hands Warm Heart
2584	Cleanliness Is Next To Godliness	2618	Cold Hard Facts
2585	Clear As A Bell	2619	Cold Shoulder
2586	Clear As Mud	2620	Cold Turkey
2587	Clear The Air	2621	Colder Than A Well Digger's Ass
2588	Clearing The Cupboard	2622	Colder Than A Witch's Tit In A Brass Bra
2589	Climb On The Bandwagon	2623	Combine Business With Pleasure
2590	Climb The Corporate Ladder	2624	Come A Callin'
2591	Climbing The Walls	2625	Come Across
2592	Cloak And Dagger Work	2626	Come Again
2593	Clock Is Ticking	2627	Come And Get It
2594	Close But No Cigar		
2595	Close Call		
2596	Close Early And Often		

2628	Come Fly With Me
2629	Come Hell Or High Water
2630	Come In Under The Wire
2631	Come On Down
2632	Come On Over
2633	Come Out Ahead Of The Game
2634	Come Out Come Out Wherever You Are
2635	Come Out Of The Closet
2636	Come Up Short
2637	Coming Apart At The Seams
2638	Coming Down In Buckets
2639	Coming Down The Pike
2640	Coming Out Of The Closet
2641	Common Sense
2642	Comparing Apples To Oranges
2643	Complete Picture
2644	Complete Picture The
2645	Confucius May Confuse Us At Times
2646	Connect The Dots
2647	Connecting All The Clues
2648	Contemplate My Navel
2649	Contrary To Popular Belief
2650	Cook One's Goose
2651	Cook With Gas
2652	Cookie Cutter
2653	Cookie Jar Accounting
2654	Cooking The Books
2655	Cooking With Gas
2656	Cool As A Cucumber
2657	Cool Moves
2658	Cool Your Heels
2659	Cool Your Jets
2660	Cop It Sweet
2661	Copy Cat
2662	Couldn't Do It To Save His Soul

2663	Couldn't Fight His Way Out Of A Wet Paper Sack
2664	Couldn't Find Your Way Out Of A Paper Bag
2665	Couldn't Make Heads Or Tails Of It
2666	Count Me In
2667	Count Your Blessings
2668	Counting His Money Like An Old Miser
2669	Course Of True Love Never Did Run Smooth
2670	Cover My Ass
2671	Covers All The Bases
2672	Coward Dies A Thousand Deaths
2673	Cowboy Up
2674	Crack Down
2675	Crack The Code
2676	Crack The Nut
2677	Crack The Whip
2678	Cracker Jack
2679	Cracking Up
2680	Crammed In Like Sardines
2681	Crap Shoot
2682	Crash And Burn
2683	Crash The Gate
2684	Crazy As A Loon
2685	Crazy As A Mad Hatter
2686	Crazy As A March Hare
2687	Crazy Like A Fox
2688	Cream Of The Crop
2689	Credit Where Credit Is Due
2690	Creme De La Creme
2691	Crib Magnet
2692	Crime Doesn't Pay
2693	Crisp And Clear
2694	Criss Cross
2695	Crocodile Tears
2696	Cross The Line

57

2697	Cross Your Heart And Hope To Die	2733	Cut To The Quick
2698	Crossing The Rubbikon	2734	Cut Your Losses
2699	Cruisin' For A Bruisin'	2735	Cut Your Teeth
2700	Cry Me A River	2736	Cute As A Bugs Ear
2701	Cry Over Spilt Milk	2737	Cute As A Button
2702	Cry Uncle	2738	Cuts Like A Knife
2703	Cry Wolf	2739	Cuts To The Core
2704	Crying All The Way To The Bank	2740	Cuts To The Quick
2705	Crying Crocodile Tears	2741	Cutting Through All The Red Tape
2706	Cup Is Either Half Empty Or Half Full	2742	Daddy Long Legs
2707	Cup Of Joe	2743	Daddy's Little Girl
2708	Curb Your Enthusiasm	2744	Dag Nabbit
2709	Curiosity Killed The Cat	2745	Dagger In The Heart
2710	Curse A Blue Streak	2746	Damn The Torpedoes Full Speed Ahead
2711	Customer Is Always Right	2747	Damned If You Do And Damned If You Don't
2712	Cut A Big Swatch	2748	Dance With The Devil
2713	Cut A Rug	2749	Dances To The Beat Of A Different Drummer
2714	Cut Above The Rest	2750	Danger Will Robinson
2715	Cut And Dry	2751	Dangle A Carrot In Front Of Him
2716	Cut And Paste	2752	Dare Devil
2717	Cut And Run	2753	Dare To Be Different
2718	Cut Corners	2754	Dark As The Night Of Day
2719	Cut From The Same Cloth	2755	Dark Horse
2720	Cut It	2756	Darkest Hour Is Just Before Dawn
2721	Cut It Out	2757	Darting To And Fro
2722	Cut Off Your Nose To Spite Your Face	2758	Dat Dawg Don't Hunt No More
2723	Cut One's Eyeteeth	2759	Dat's A Lot
2724	Cut Out The Middleman	2760	Dat's All Folks
2725	Cut The Bull	2761	David Versus Goliath
2726	Cut The Cheese	2762	Davy Jones's Locker
2727	Cut The Dead Wood	2763	Day Late And A Dollar Short
2728	Cut The Mustard	2764	Day To Day Operation
2729	Cut The Rug	2765	Days Of Wine & Roses The
2730	Cut Them Down To Size		
2731	Cut Through All The Red Tape		
2732	Cut To The Chase		

58

2766	Days Of Wine And Roses
2767	Dazed And Confused
2768	De Plane - De Plane
2769	Dead As A Dodo Bird
2770	Dead As A Doornail
2771	Dead As A Herring
2772	Dead Cats Bounce
2773	Dead In The Water
2774	Dead Men Never Bite
2775	Dead Men Tell No Tales
2776	Dead On Arrival
2777	Dead Presidents
2778	Dead Ringer
2779	Dead To Rights
2780	Deaf As A Post
2781	Deal With It
2782	Dealing From The Bottom Of The Deck
2783	Dealt A Fatal Blow
2784	Death Before Dishonor
2785	Death By A Thousand Cuts
2786	Death Is A Great Leveler
2787	Death Is A Once In A Lifetime Experience
2788	Deeds Not Words
2789	Deep Do Do
2790	Deep In Thought
2791	Deep Pockets
2792	Deep Six
2793	Deep Six Someone
2794	Delivered To You On A Silver Platter
2795	Delve A Little Deeper
2796	Denny Crane
2797	Desperate Times Call For Desperate Measures
2798	Devil To Pay
2799	Devil's Advocate
2800	Dial Up
2801	Diamond In The Rough

2802	Diamonds Are A Girls Best Friend
2803	Dicey Situation
2804	Did Your Level Best
2805	Diddly Squat
2806	Didn't Like The Color Of His Money
2807	Die Hard
2808	Die Is Cast
2809	Die With Your Boots On
2810	Different Strokes For Different Folks
2811	Dig Deep Down
2812	Dig For Gold
2813	Dig The Well Before You're Thirsty
2814	Dig Yourself Into A Hole
2815	Ding A Ling
2816	Ding Bat
2817	Ding Dong
2818	Ding Dong The Witch Is Dead
2819	Dip Your Toe In The Water
2820	Dipped In Honey
2821	Dirt Cheap
2822	Dirt Don't Hurt
2823	Discretion Is The Better Part Of Valor
2824	Display The Power
2825	Distance Makes The Heart Grow Fonder
2826	Divide And Conquer
2827	Do A One Eighty
2828	Do As I Say And Not As I Do
2829	Do Birds Fly
2830	Do It For Yourself
2831	Do It Now
2832	Do It Today
2833	Do It Yourself
2834	Do Not Disturb

2835	Do Not Forward	2867	Dog Eat Dog
2836	Do Or Die	2868	Dog Gone
2837	Do Or Don't	2869	Dog It
2838	Do Something Brilliant	2870	Dog Tired
2839	Do Something Drastic	2871	Doggin' It
2840	Do The Dutch	2872	Dogs Bark But The Caravan Moves On
2841	Do The Wild Mambo		
2842	Do Unto Others As You Would Have Other Do Unto You	2873	Dogs Bollocks
		2874	Dogs Have Masters Cats Have Staff
2843	Do What It Takes	2875	Dog's Life
2844	Do Ya Think I'm Sexy	2876	Doing The Horizontal Bop
2845	Do You Believe	2877	Doing Time
2846	Do You Copy	2878	Doing Well By Doing Good
2847	Do You Feel Lucky	2879	Don't Ask Me No Questions
2848	Do You Feel Me		
2849	Do You Know What I Mean	2880	Don't Be Cruel
2850	Do You Think I'm Made Of Money	2881	Don't Be Stupid
		2882	Don't Bring Me Down
2851	Do You Want The Good News Or The Bad News First	2883	Don't Get Hooked On Me
		2884	Don't Stop
		2885	Don't Think Twice It's Alright
2852	Do Your Homework		
2853	Do Your Research	2886	Done Up Like A Christmas Tree
2854	Dodging It		
2855	Does A Bear Shit In The Woods	2887	Don't Add Insult To Injury
		2888	Don't Air Your Dirty Laundry In Public
2856	Does It Really Matter		
2857	Does Not Compute	2889	Don't Bat Your Eyelashes At Me Buster
2858	Does That Ring A Bell		
2859	Does The Pope Wear A Funny Hat	2890	Don't Be A Butthead
		2891	Don't Be A Nincompoop
2860	Doesn't Have Both Oars In The Water	2892	Don't Be A One-Note Johnny
		2893	Don't Be A Party Pooper
2861	Doesn't Know If She's Washing Or Hanging Out	2894	Don't Be A Stick In The Mud
		2895	Don't Be Caught Flat Footed
2862	Doesn't Really Matter Does It		
		2896	Don't Be Penny Wise And Dollar Foolish
2863	Doesn't Stand A Chance		
2864	Doesn't Stand A Prayer	2897	Don't Be Stupid
2865	Dog And Pony		
2866	Dog Day Afternoon		

60

2898	Don't Be Such A Big Girl's Blouse	2921	Don't Drink The Kool Aid
2899	Don't Believe Everything You Hear	2922	Don't Drop The Ball
		2923	Don't Even Bother
		2924	Don't Even Try
2900	Don't Bite Off More Than You Can Chew	2925	Don't Fall For That Old Trick
2901	Don't Bite The Hand That Feeds You	2926	Don't Fall For That One
		2927	Don't Fall Into That Trap
2902	Don't Build Castles In The Air	2928	Don't Fire 'Til You See The Whites Of Their Eyes
2903	Don't Burn All Of Your Bridges	2929	Don't Fly Off The Handle
		2930	Don't Forget
2904	Don't Burn The Bridges Behind You	2931	Don't Forget To Eat Your Veggies
2905	Don't Burn Your Candles At Both Ends	2932	Don't Get Conned
		2933	Don't Get In An Uproar
2906	Don't Buy A Pig In A Poke	2934	Don't Get Mad Get Even
2907	Don't Call Us We'll Call You	2935	Don't Get Overwhelmed
2908	Don't Change Horses In Midstream	2936	Don't Get Your Knickers In A Knot
2909	Don't Change The Rules In The Middle Of The Game	2937	Don't Get Your Knickers In A Twist
2910	Don't Come The Raw Prawn With Me	2938	Don't Get Your Panties In A Bunch
2911	Don't Count Your Chickens Before They Cross The Road	2939	Don't Get Your Panties In A Wad
2912	Don't Count Your Chickens Before They're Hatched	2940	Don't Give It A Second Thought
2913	Don't Count Your Chickens Till The Cows Come Home	2941	Don't Give Up
		2942	Don't Give Up The Ship
2914	Don't Cross The Bridge Until You Come To It	2943	Don't Go Down There
		2944	Don't Go There
2915	Don't Cry In My Beer	2945	Don't Have A Cow
2916	Don't Cry Over Spilt Milk	2946	Don't Have Too Many Irons In The Fire
2917	Don't Cut Off Your Nose To Spite Your Face	2947	Don't Have Two Nickels To Rub Together
2918	Don't Dig Yourself Into A Hole	2948	Don't Hide Your Light Under A Bushel
2919	Don't Dilly Dally	2949	Don't Hit A Man When He's Down
2920	Don't Do Anything I Wouldn't Do		

2950	Don't Hold Your Breath
2951	Don't Jingle Jangle
2952	Don't Judge A Book By It's Cover
2953	Don't Judge A Man Until You've Walked A Mile In His Boots
2954	Don't Jump From The Frying Pan Into The Fire
2955	Don't Jump To Conclusions
2956	Don't Kill The Goose That Laid The Golden Egg
2957	Don't Know Beans About
2958	Don't Know Him From Adam
2959	Don't Know Jack
2960	Don't Know Shit From Shinola
2961	Don't Lead With Your Chin
2962	Don't Let The Bedbugs Bite
2963	Don't Let The Fox Guard The Hen House
2964	Don't Let The Grass Grow Under Your Feet
2965	Don't Look A Gift Horse In The Mouth
2966	Don't Look Back
2967	Don't Make A Fuss
2968	Don't Make A Mountain Out Of A Molehill
2969	Don't Make It A Federal Case
2970	Don't Make Me Angry
2971	Don't Make Me Come Over There
2972	Don't Make Me Do Something I'll Regret
2973	Don't Make The Same Mistake Twice
2974	Don't Miss Out
2975	Don't Miss The Boat

2976	Don't Monkey With It
2977	Don't Paint The Devil On The Wall
2978	Don't Paint Yourself Into A Corner
2979	Don't Pee On My Leg And Tell Me It's Raining
2980	Don't Piss Into The Wind
2981	Don't Piss On The Chips
2982	Don't Play With Fire
2983	Don't Play With Your Food
2984	Don't Pour New Wine In Old Bottles
2985	Don't Pull My Leg
2986	Don't Push Your Luck
2987	Don't Put All Your Eggs In One Basket
2988	Don't Put Off Till Tomorrow What You Can Do Today
2989	Don't Put The Cart Before The Horse
2990	Don't Put Words In My Mouth
2991	Don't Quit Your Day Job
2992	Don't Rain On My Parade
2993	Don't Read This
2994	Don't Reinvent The Wheel
2995	Don't Rock The Boat
2996	Don't Sell Yourself Short
2997	Don't Shoot Me I'm Just The Messenger
2998	Don't Shoot The Messenger
2999	Don't Shout Until You're Out Of The Woods
3000	Don't Spill The Beans
3001	Don't Spit Into The Wind
3002	Don't Spread Yourself Too Thin
3003	Don't Start Anything You Can't Finish

3004	Don't Step On Other People's Toes
3005	Don't Stick Your Neck Out
3006	Don't Stop The Music
3007	Don't Stop There
3008	Don't Sweat It
3009	Don't Sweat The Small Things
3010	Don't Take Any Wooden Nickels
3011	Don't Take The Name Of The Lord In Vain
3012	Don't Tell Tall Tales
3013	Don't Tempt Fate
3014	Don't Throw A Monkey Wrench Into The Works
3015	Don't Throw Out The Baby With The Bath Water
3016	Don't Throw Your Pearls Before Swine
3017	Don't Toot Your Own Horn
3018	Don't Touch That
3019	Don't Trash This
3020	Don't Tread On Me
3021	Don't Trust The Lock To Which Everyone Has A Key
3022	Don't Try To Hoodwink Me
3023	Don't Try To Rip Me Off
3024	Don't Try To Teach Your Grandmother To Suck Eggs
3025	Don't Upset The Apple Cart
3026	Don't Use A Lot Where A Little Will Do
3027	Don't Wait Until You Find Yourself Behind The 8 Ball
3028	Don't Want To Cover Old Ground
3029	Don't Wash Your Dirty Laundry In Public
3030	Don't Wear Your Heart On Your Sleeve

3031	Doodle Bug
3032	Dos And Don'ts
3033	Dose Of Reality
3034	Dot Your I's And Cross Your T's
3035	Dot's A Lot Of Moolah
3036	Dots All Folks
3037	Double Crossed
3038	Double Dog Dare Ya
3039	Double Double Toil And Trouble
3040	Double Entendre
3041	Double Jeopardy
3042	Double Or Nothing
3043	Double Whammy
3044	Dough Boy
3045	Down And Out
3046	Down In The Dumps
3047	Down In The Mouth
3048	Down Memory Lane
3049	Down On Your Luck
3050	Down The Hatch
3051	Down Time
3052	Down To Business
3053	Down To Earth
3054	Down To The Wire
3055	Dr Jekyll And Mr. Hyde
3056	Dr Livingstone I Presume
3057	Dragged Out Kicking And Screaming
3058	Drain The Lizard
3059	Draw A Blank
3060	Draw A Line In The Sand
3061	Drawing A Long Bow
3062	Dream Big
3063	Dream Car
3064	Dream On
3065	Dream The Impossible
3066	Dreams Come True
3067	Dressed Better Than Sunday

3068	Dressed To Kill
3069	Dressed To The Nines
3070	Drive It Home
3071	Drive Me Nuts
3072	Drive Me To Drink
3073	Drive Me Up A Wall
3074	Drive The Point Home
3075	Drive The Porcelain Bus
3076	Drive Them Up A Wall
3077	Drives You Nuts
3078	Driving Me Crazy
3079	Driving The Porcelain Bus
3080	Driving Your Ducks To A Mighty Pond
3081	Drop A Dime
3082	Drop And Give Me 10
3083	Drop In The Bucket
3084	Drop Me A Line
3085	Drop The Ball
3086	Drop The Hammer
3087	Dropped Dead In My Tracks
3088	Dropping Like Flies
3089	Dropping The Ball
3090	Drown Your Sorrows
3091	Drowning In Your Sorrows
3092	Drum Up Support
3093	Drunk As A Fiddler
3094	Drunk As A Skunk
3095	Dry As A Bone
3096	Duck It
3097	Duck Soup
3098	Ducky Doo
3099	Dude This Is Serious
3100	Dum Dum Bullet
3101	Dumb As A Post
3102	Dumb As A Stump
3103	Dumb Like A Fox
3104	Dumber Than A Bag Of Hammers
3105	Dumber Than A Box Of Rocks

3106	Dust In The Wind
3107	Dutch Auction
3108	Dutch Treat
3109	Duty Calls
3110	Dyed In The Wool
3111	Dyn-O-Mite
3112	E Pluribus Unum
3113	Eager Beaver
3114	Early Bird Catches The Worm
3115	Early To Bed Early To Rise Makes A Man Healthy Wealthy And Wise
3116	Earmark This
3117	Earn One's Stripes
3118	Earned His Wings
3119	Ease His Pain
3120	Ease Of Use
3121	Ease Their Minds
3122	Easier Said Than Done
3123	Easier Than Government Work
3124	East Is East And West Is West
3125	Easy As 123
3126	Easy As ABC
3127	Easy As Falling Off A Log
3128	Easy As Pie
3129	Easy As Rolling Off A Log
3130	Easy As That
3131	Easy Come And Easy Go
3132	Easy Does It
3133	Easy Money
3134	Easy To Acquire
3135	Easy To Follow
3136	Easy To Implement
3137	Easy To Understand
3138	Easy To Use
3139	Eat All Your Food There Are Children Starving In China

3140	Eat Crow
3141	Eat Dirt
3142	Eat Drink And Be Merry
3143	Eat Humble Pie
3144	Eat Lead
3145	Eat My Dust
3146	Eat My Hat
3147	Eat My Shorts
3148	Eat One's Words
3149	Eat To Live Do Not Live To Eat
3150	Eat Your Gun
3151	Eat Your Heart Out
3152	Eat Your Own Dog Food
3153	Eat Your Vegetables
3154	Eating Dog Food
3155	Eating Humble Pie
3156	Eats Like A Horse
3157	Eats Like A Thrashing Machine
3158	Eaves Dropper
3159	Eeny Meany Money Moe
3160	Egg On Your Face
3161	Eight Days A Week
3162	Eight Hundred Pound Gorilla
3163	Elbow Grease
3164	Elementary My Dear Watson
3165	Elephant In The Room
3166	Eleventh Hour
3167	Emotional Roller Coaster
3168	Emphasize The Wrong Syllable
3169	Empty Flattery
3170	Empty Promises And Broken Dreams
3171	Empty Versus Full
3172	End Justifies The Means
3173	End Of One's Rope
3174	End Of The Line

3175	End Of The Road
3176	End Over End
3177	Ends Justify The Means
3178	Enjoy The Easy Life
3179	Enjoy The Freedom
3180	Enjoy The Moment
3181	Enjoy The Ride
3182	Enough Is Enough
3183	Enough Money To Burn A Wet Dog
3184	Enter The Lions Den
3185	Entering Uncharted Waters
3186	Erase Your Doubts
3187	Essentially Is Essentially Meaningless
3188	ET Phone Home
3189	Et Tu Brute
3190	Etched In My Mind
3191	Eureka
3192	Even A Blind Pig Occasionally Picks Up An Acorn
3193	Even A Blind Sow Gets An Acorn Every Now And Then
3194	Even A Blind Squirrel Finds An Acorn Once In A While
3195	Even A Worm Will Turn
3196	Even Keel
3197	Even Money
3198	Even Stevens
3199	Even The Sun Shines On A Dogs Ass Some Days
3200	Every Cloud Has A Silver Lining
3201	Every Dark Cloud Has A Silver Lining
3202	Every Day Is A Winding Road
3203	Every Dog Has His Day
3204	Every Employee Rises To His Level Of Incompetence
3205	Every Little Bit Helps

3206	Every Man For Himself	3232	Everything To Gain
3207	Every Man Has His Price	3233	Everything's Coming Up Daisies
3208	Every Man Has Stupid Thoughts-Wise Men Keep Them Quiet	3234	Everything's Coming Up Roses
3209	Every Man Is His Own Worst Enemy	3235	Everything's Copasetic
		3236	Everything's Hunky Dory
3210	Every Man Is The Architect Of His Own Fortune	3237	Everything's Under Control
		3238	Evil To Him Who Evil Thinks
3211	Every Man Makes Mistakes	3239	Exception Proves The Rule
3212	Every Man To His Own Taste	3240	Excited As A Bucket Of Warm Spit
3213	Every Rose Has It's Thorn	3241	Exclusive Offer
3214	Every Second Is Critical	3242	Expect The Best
3215	Every Time A Bell Rings An Angel Get Its Wings	3243	Experience Is The Best Teacher
3216	Every Tom Dick & Harry	3244	Experience The Difference
3217	Every Wall Is A Door	3245	Experts Are Predicting
		3246	Experts Have Predicted
3218	Every Which Way But Loose	3247	Explained In Detail
		3248	Explained in Full
3219	Everybody Is Wise After The Event	3249	Explore Your Options
		3250	Extremes Meet
3220	Everybody Loves Somebody	3251	Eye Carumba
3221	Everybody Plays The Fool	3252	Eye For An Eye And A For A Tooth
3222	Everybody's Doing It	3253	Eye To Eye
3223	Everyone Has His 15 Minutes Of Fame	3254	Eyeball Someone Or Something
3224	Everyone Has Their Cross To Bear	3255	Eyeball To Eyeball
3225	Everyone Makes Mistakes	3256	Eyes Are The Mirrors Of The Soul
3226	Everything But The Kitchen Sink	3257	Face Like A Bag Of Spanners
3227	Everything Comes Out In The Wash	3258	Face Like A Bulldog Chewing On A Wasp
3228	Everything Falls Into Place	3259	Face Like A Burst Couch
3229	Everything Happens To Me	3260	Face Like A Dropped Meat Pie
3230	Everything Is Not All Peaches And Cream	3261	Face Only A Mother Could Love
3231	Everything Old Is New Again		

66

3262	Face That Would Scare A Dog Out Of A Butcher Shop
3263	Face The Music
3264	Face Up To The Facts
3265	Fact Is Stranger Than Fiction
3266	Facts And Figures
3267	Facts Are Facts
3268	Facts Logic Reasons And Solutions Sell
3269	Fail To Plan Is A Plan To Fail
3270	Faint Heart Never A True Love Knows
3271	Fair Haired One
3272	Fair To Middling
3273	Fair Weather Friend
3274	Faith Can Move Mountains
3275	Fake It Till You Make It
3276	Fall Guy
3277	Fall Head Over Heels
3278	Fall Off The Wagon
3279	Fall Through The Cracks
3280	Falling Off A Log Is Easy As
3281	Familiarity Breeds Contempt
3282	Family Affair
3283	Family That Prays Together Stays Together
3284	Fan Fare
3285	Fan The Flames
3286	Fancy Meeting You Here
3287	Fancy Pancy
3288	Fancy Pants
3289	Fantastic Savings
3290	Fantasy Island
3291	Far And Away The Best
3292	Far Cry
3293	Fashion Victim
3294	Fast And Cheap
3295	Fast Buck
3296	Fast Start Up
3297	Fast To Act
3298	Fasten Your Seat Belts
3299	Fasten Your Seatbelt It's Going To Be A Bumpy Ride
3300	Faster Better Cheaper
3301	Faster Than A Speeding Bullet
3302	Faster Than Grease Lightning
3303	Fat As A Cow
3304	Fat As A Pig
3305	Fat Chance
3306	Fat Is In The Fire
3307	Fat Lip
3308	Father Knows Best
3309	Father Time
3310	Fear Of Failure
3311	Feast Your Eyes On This
3312	Feather In His Cap
3313	Feather In Your Cap
3314	Feather Your Own Nest
3315	Fed Up
3316	Federal Case
3317	Feed A Cold Starve A Fever
3318	Feel Like 16 Again
3319	Feel Like A Fifth Wheel
3320	Feel The Power
3321	Feelin' So Good
3322	Fell Off My Plate
3323	Fell Off The Wagon
3324	Few Bricks Shy
3325	Few Fries Short Of A Happy Meal
3326	Few Sandwiches Short Of A Picnic
3327	Fewer And Far Between
3328	Fickle Finger Of Fate
3329	Fiddle De De
3330	Fiddle Faddle
3331	Fiddle Sticks

67

3332	Fiddling While Rome Burns
3333	Fifth Wheel
3334	Fifty-Fifty
3335	Fifty-Fifty Chance
3336	Fifty-Fifty Proposition
3337	Fight Fire With Fire
3338	Fight Like A Man
3339	Fight Like Cats And Dogs
3340	Figure It Out
3341	Figures Don't Lie
3342	Fill In For Someone
3343	Fill In The Gaps
3344	Fill Your Hope Chest
3345	Filthy Rich
3346	Finally A Solution To Poverty
3347	Finally It's Here
3348	Finally It's Ready
3349	Find A Match
3350	Finders Keepers Losers Weepers
3351	Finding The Truth
3352	Fine And Dandy
3353	Fine As Wine
3354	Fine Line
3355	Finer Than Frog Hair
3356	Fingered
3357	Fingers Were Made Before Forks
3358	Fire And Ice
3359	Fire In The Belly
3360	Fire In The Hole
3361	Fire Your Boss
3362	Fired Up Yet
3363	Firing On All Cylinders
3364	First 100 Years Are The Hardest
3365	First Catch Your Rabbit Then Make Your Stew
3366	First Class Operation
3367	First Come First Served

3368	First Comes Love Then Comes Marriage
3369	First Do No Harm
3370	First Impressions Are The Most Lasting
3371	First In Last Out
3372	First Rate
3373	First Step Is The Hardest
3374	First The Good News
3375	First Things First
3376	Fish In Troubled Waters
3377	Fish Or Cut Bait
3378	Fish Out Of Water
3379	Fish Where The Fish Are
3380	Fit As A Fiddle
3381	Fit To Be Hung
3382	Fit To Be Tied
3383	Fit's Any Budget
3384	Fits Like A Glove
3385	Fits Like A Hand In A Glove
3386	Fixing A Hole
3387	Flabbergast
3388	Flag Someone Down
3389	Flash As A Rat With A Gold Tooth
3390	Flash In The Pan
3391	Flat As A Board
3392	Flat As A Long Poured Champagne
3393	Flat As A Pancake
3394	Flat On Your Back
3395	Flattery Will Get You Nowhere
3396	Flea Bitten
3397	Flea In One's Ear
3398	Fleet Footed
3399	Fleet Of Foot
3400	Flew The Coup
3401	Flights Of Fantasy
3402	Flim Flam
3403	Flip Flop

68

3404	Flip Your Lid
3405	Flipped Her Lid
3406	Flippin The Bird
3407	Flirt With Disaster
3408	Flog A Dead Horse
3409	Flogging A Dead Horse
3410	Flop House
3411	Flowers Leave Fragrance In The Hand That Bestowed Them
3412	Flown The Coop
3413	Fly By Night
3414	Fly By The Book
3415	Fly By The Seat Of Your Pants
3416	Fly In The Face
3417	Fly In The Ointment
3418	Fly Like An Eagle
3419	Fly Me To The Moon
3420	Fly Off The Handle
3421	Fly On The Wall
3422	Fly Straight
3423	Fly The Coop
3424	Fly With Eagles
3425	Flying Blindfold
3426	Flying Buttress
3427	Flying By The Seat Of Your Pants
3428	Foaming At The Mouth
3429	Follow In My Footsteps
3430	Follow Me
3431	Follow Suit
3432	Follow That Dream
3433	Follow The Bouncing Ball
3434	Follow The Leader
3435	Following In His Footsteps
3436	Food For Thought
3437	Fool And His Money Are Soon Parted
3438	Fool Me Once Shame On You

3439	Fool Me Once Shame On You Fool Me Twice Shame On Me
3440	Fool Me Twice Shame On Me
3441	Fools Gold
3442	Fools Rush In
3443	Fools Rush In Where Angels Fear To Tread
3444	Foot Loose And Fancy Free
3445	Foot The Bill
3446	Footloose And Fancy Free
3447	Footprints On The Sands Of Time
3448	For Crying Out Loud
3449	For Every Honest Man - Name Another Who Tells The Truth
3450	For Everyday People
3451	For Everything There Is A Season
3452	For God's Sake
3453	For Goodness Sake
3454	For He's A Jolly Good Fellow
3455	For Love Or Money
3456	For Once In My Life
3457	For Pete's Sake
3458	For The Birds
3459	For The First Time
3460	For The Good Times
3461	For The Love Of Pete
3462	For Want Of A Nail The Kingdom Was Lost
3463	For Want Of The Nail A Shoe Was Lost
3464	For What It's Worth
3465	For What It's Worth
3466	For Whom The Bell Tolls
3467	Forbidden Fruit Is Sweet
3468	Forever And A Day
3469	Forever And Ever Amen

3470	Forewarned Is Forearmed
3471	Forged In The Heat Of Battle
3472	Forget About It
3473	Forget Me Not
3474	Forget The Hype
3475	Forget The Junk
3476	Forgive And Forget
3477	Fork It Over
3478	Fork Out
3479	Form A Loose Grip
3480	Fortune Favors The Brave
3481	Fortune Favors The Strong The Rich And The Famous
3482	Forty Winks
3483	Fountain Of Youth
3484	Four On The Floor
3485	Four One One
3486	Frankly My Dear I Don't Give A Damn
3487	Free As A Bird
3488	Free Bird
3489	Free For All
3490	Free From The Daily Grind
3491	Free Of Charge
3492	Free Reign
3493	Free Ride
3494	Free Test Drive
3495	Free To You
3496	Freedom Is Never Free
3497	Frequently Asked Questions
3498	Fresh As A Daisy
3499	Fresh Out Of Ideas
3500	Fresh Out Of Water
3501	Frick And Frack
3502	Fried To One's Tonsils
3503	Friend In Need Is A Friend Indeed
3504	Friend Or Foe
3505	Friends Never Say

	Goodbye
3506	Friendship Is The Only Cement Holding The World Together
3507	Frightened Of New Ideas I'm Frightened By The Old Ones
3508	Frisky As A Puppy
3509	Frog In My Throat
3510	From A Whole New Point Of View
3511	From Day One
3512	From Here To Timbuktu
3513	From Little Acorns Great Oaks Grow
3514	From Many One
3515	From Pillar To Post
3516	From Point A To Point B
3517	From Rags To Riches
3518	From The Beginning
3519	From The Bottom Of My Heart
3520	From The Four Corners Of The Earth
3521	From The Frying Pan Into The Fire
3522	From The Get Go
3523	From The Mouths Of Babes Come Words Of Wisdom
3524	From This Moment On
3525	From Your Lips To God's Ears
3526	Frozen Assets
3527	Fuel To Fire
3528	Full Monty
3529	Full Of Beans
3530	Full Of Himself
3531	Full Of Hot Air
3532	Full Of It
3533	Full Of Mischief
3534	Full Of The Devil
3535	Full Of Vinegar

3536	Full Speed Ahead
3537	Full To The Back Teeth
3538	Full Versus Empty
3539	Funny As A Barrel Of Monkeys
3540	Funny Bone
3541	Funny Business
3542	Funny Face
3543	Funny Money
3544	Funny You Mention It
3545	Fur Coat And No Knickers
3546	Gadzooks
3547	Gag Me With A Spoon
3548	Game Is On The Line
3549	Gang Bang
3550	Gang Bangers
3551	Gang Plank
3552	Garbage In Garbage Out
3553	Garlic Milkshake
3554	Gather Ye Rosebuds While Ye May
3555	Gathering Like Flies
3556	Gave It A Wide Berth
3557	Gee Mrs. Cleaver
3558	Genius Is Born Not Made
3559	Genius Is The Infinite Capacity For Taking Pains
3560	Gentlemen Prefer Blondes
3561	Gentlemen Start Your Engines
3562	Get A Grip
3563	Get A Grip On Yourself
3564	Get A Handle On This
3565	Get A Head Start
3566	Get A Kick Out Of It
3567	Get A Leg Up
3568	Get A Life
3569	Get A Room
3570	Get A Word In Edgewise
3571	Get Ahead Early And Stay Ahead Late

3572	Get All Worked Up
3573	Get Along Like Oil And Water
3574	Get An Earful
3575	Get Back Up On The Horse
3576	Get Cleaned Out
3577	Get Crushed
3578	Get Down
3579	Get Down To Bare Bones
3580	Get Down To Brass Tacks
3581	Get Down To The Nitty Gritty
3582	Get Down Tonight
3583	Get In Your Hair
3584	Get It
3585	Get It Done
3586	Get It Outta My Hair
3587	Get It While It's Hot
3588	Get Lost
3589	Get My Drift
3590	Get My Message
3591	Get Off
3592	Get Off My Plane
3593	Get Off Your High Horse
3594	Get On Her Soap Box
3595	Get On The Bandwagon
3596	Get On Your High Horse
3597	Get One's Goat
3598	Get Out And Stay Out
3599	Get Out Of Dodge
3600	Get Out Of Here
3601	Get Out Of My Hair
3602	Get Out Of The Sack And Get To Work
3603	Get Outta Town By Sundown
3604	Get Over The Hump
3605	Get Started Today
3606	Get Stuffed
3607	Get The Ball Rolling
3608	Get The Best

71

3609	Get The Brush Off
3610	Get The Drop On You
3611	Get The Facts
3612	Get The Hook
3613	Get The Lead Out
3614	Get The Money
3615	Get The Peanut Butter Out Of Your Ears
3616	Get The Picture
3617	Get The Red Carpet Treatment
3618	Get The Sack
3619	Get The Scoop
3620	Get The Show On The Road
3621	Get The Star Treatment
3622	Get The Third Degree
3623	Get To The Bottom Of It
3624	Get Up Off The Mat
3625	Get With The Program
3626	Get Your Act Together
3627	Get Your Arms Around It
3628	Get Your Dander Up
3629	Get Your Ducks In A Row
3630	Get Your Feet Wet
3631	Get Your Foot In The Door
3632	Get Your Goat
3633	Get Your Head In The Game
3634	Get Your Stinking Paws Off Me
3635	Gets My Dander Up
3636	Getting A Foothold
3637	Getting Ahead Of The Game
3638	Getting All Your Ducks In A Row
3639	Getting Blood From A Stone
3640	Getting Cleaned Out
3641	Getting Cold Feet
3642	Getting Down To Grass Roots
3643	Getting Hitched
3644	Getting On Her High Horse
3645	Getting One Up On The Competition
3646	Getting To Be An Old Hand At It
3647	Getting Up To Speed
3648	Giddy Up
3649	Gift Of Gab
3650	Gilded Lilly
3651	Gimme A Break
3652	Gird Your Loins
3653	Girls Just Wanna Have Fun
3654	Girls Will Be Girls
3655	Give A Beggar A Horse And He'll Ride It To Death
3656	Give A Hoot
3657	Give A Lick And A Promise
3658	Give A Little Take A Little
3659	Give A Man A Fish And You'll Feed Him For A Day
3660	Give A Wide Berth
3661	Give An Inch And He Takes A Mile
3662	Give And Take
3663	Give Credit Where Credit Is Due
3664	Give 'Em Hell Harry
3665	Give Him A Run For His Money
3666	Give Him An Inch And He'll Take A Mile
3667	Give Him Enough Rope And He'll Hang Himself
3668	Give It A Rest
3669	Give It A Whirl
3670	Give It Away
3671	Give It The Old College Try
3672	Give Me A Break
3673	Give Me A Hand
3674	Give Me A Place To Stand And I'll Move The Earth

72

3675	Give Me Five Minutes
3676	Give Me Liberty Or Give Me Death
3677	Give Me Your Tired And Your Poor
3678	Give Me Your Two-Cents Worth
3679	Give Peace A Chance
3680	Give Someone A Hand
3681	Give The Shirt Off Your Back
3682	Give Them A Finger And They'll Take The Whole Hand
3683	Give Them A Hand
3684	Give Them An Inch And They'll Take A Mile
3685	Give Your Right Arm
3686	Give Yourself A Right Hand Ring
3687	Given To Him On A Silver Platter
3688	Giving Them The Third Degree
3689	Glad To Help
3690	Glass Is Either Half Empty Or Half Full
3691	Glimmer Of Hope
3692	Gloss Over
3693	Glowing Like A Good Deed In A Naughty World
3694	Glutton For Punishment
3695	Go Against The Grain
3696	Go Ahead Make My Day
3697	Go Away And Leave Me Alone
3698	Go Back To The Well
3699	Go Ballistic
3700	Go Belly Up
3701	Go Berserk
3702	Go Crazy
3703	Go Do Your Homework
3704	Go Down Hill
3705	Go Down The Garden Path
3706	Go Down The Pike
3707	Go Figure
3708	Go Fly A Kite
3709	Go For All The Marbles
3710	Go For Broke
3711	Go For It
3712	Go For It All
3713	Go Haywire
3714	Go Head To Head
3715	Go Hog Wild
3716	Go Jump In The Lake
3717	Go Off Half Cocked
3718	Go Off The Deep End
3719	Go On Just Ask Her Out
3720	Go Out In A Blaze Of Glory
3721	Go Out On A Limb
3722	Go Over His Head
3723	Go Overboard
3724	Go Postal
3725	Go Right Ahead
3726	Go Scot Free
3727	Go The Extra Mile
3728	Go Through The Motions
3729	Go Through The Roof
3730	Go To Guys
3731	Go To Rack And Ruin
3732	Go To The Dickens
3733	Go To The Thumbs
3734	Go To The Wall
3735	Go Together Hand In Hand
3736	Go Too Far
3737	Go West Young Man
3738	Go Where The Green Lights Lead You
3739	Go Whole Hog
3740	Go With It
3741	Go With The Flow
3742	Go With Your Gut

73

3743	Gobble De Gook
3744	Gobsmacked
3745	God Bless America
3746	God Bless The Child
3747	God Bless You
3748	God Help Us
3749	God Helps Those Who Help Themselves
3750	God Is In The Details
3751	God Moves In A Mysterious Way
3752	God Only Knows
3753	God Speed
3754	God Willing And The Creek Don't Rise
3755	God Works In Mysterious Ways
3756	God'll Get Your For That
3757	Godsend
3758	Going Against The Grain
3759	Going Against The Tide
3760	Going All The Way
3761	Going All The Way To The Top
3762	Going Bananas
3763	Going Gang Busters
3764	Going Going Gone
3765	Going In One Ear And Out The Other
3766	Going Out Head First
3767	Going Out Of Business
3768	Going The Extra Mile
3769	Going To Hell In A Hand Basket
3770	Going To The Dogs
3771	Going To Town
3772	Gold Digger
3773	Golden Child
3774	Golly Gee Willikers
3775	Gone But Not Forgotten
3776	Gone Crazy
3777	Gone Haywire
3778	Gone He Is
3779	Gone To Pot
3780	Gone To The Dogs
3781	Gone With The Wind
3782	Good As Gold
3783	Good As New
3784	Good Beginning Is Half The Battle
3785	Good Beginning Makes A Good Ending
3786	Good Bye
3787	Good Call
3788	Good Crack
3789	Good Egg
3790	Good Fences Make Good Neighbors
3791	Good Grief
3792	Good Is The Enemy Of Great
3793	Good Luck
3794	Good Luck Charm
3795	Good Man Is Hard To Find
3796	Good Morning Vietnam
3797	Good News
3798	Good News Begets Good News
3799	Good Night And Good Luck
3800	Good Night John Boy
3801	Good One
3802	Good Reputation Is More Valuable Than Money
3803	Good Riddance To Bad Rubbish
3804	Good Rule Of Thumb
3805	Good Soldier
3806	Good Things Come To Those Who Wait
3807	Good To Go
3808	Good To The Last Drop
3809	Goodie Two Shoes

74

3810	Goody Goody Gumdrops
3811	Goody Two Shoes
3812	Goofing Off
3813	Got A Hole In His Pocket
3814	Got A Leg Up
3815	Got A Leg Up On It
3816	Got A Loaf In The Oven
3817	Got A Minute
3818	Got Beat Like A Drum
3819	Got Burned
3820	Got Him By The Short Hairs
3821	Got Knocked Up
3822	Got Lost In The Shuffle
3823	Got My Mojo Workin'
3824	Got Off On The Wrong Foot
3825	Got Schooled
3826	Got Spanked
3827	Got Swept
3828	Got Taken For A Ride
3829	Got The Message
3830	Got The Stuffing Beat Out Of Him
3831	Got Them By The Short And Curlies
3832	Got To Be Crazy
3833	Got To Run
3834	Got To Run Now
3835	Got Under My Skin
3836	Got Whooped
3837	Got You Over A Barrel
3838	Got Your Hand Caught In The Cookie Jar
3839	Got Your Head In The Clouds
3840	Got Your Nose All Pushed Out Of Joint
3841	Gotcha
3842	Gotta Blast
3843	Gotting Off On The Right Foot

3844	Government Of The People By The People And For The People
3845	Grab A Bite
3846	Grab A Piece Of The Pie
3847	Grasping At Straws
3848	Grass Is Always Greener On The Other Side Of The Fence
3849	Graveyard Shift
3850	Grease A Palm
3851	Grease Lightning
3852	Great Minds Collide
3853	Great Minds Think Alike
3854	Greatest Thing Since Sliced Bread
3855	Greed For Lack Of A Better Word Is Good
3856	Green Eyed Monster
3857	Green Green Grass Of Home
3858	Green Horn
3859	Green With Envy
3860	Greener Pastures
3861	Grey Hairs
3862	Grin And Bear It
3863	Grin Like A Cheshire Cat
3864	Grinning From Ear To Ear
3865	Grist For The Mill
3866	Ground Floor Opportunity
3867	Ground Hog
3868	Ground Rules
3869	Ground Zero
3870	Groundhog Day
3871	Growing Like A Weed
3872	Growing Like Mad
3873	Grub Street
3874	Guilty Conscience Needs No Accuser
3875	Gum Up The Works
3876	Gung Ho

75

3877	Gunning For
3878	Guns Blazing
3879	Guns Don't Kill People Do
3880	Gut Check
3881	Habits Decide Character
3882	Hail To The Chief
3883	Hair Of The Dog
3884	Half A Bubble Off
3885	Half A Loaf Is Better Than None
3886	Half Baked Idea
3887	Half Cocked
3888	Half The Battle
3889	Hall Mark
3890	Ham It Up
3891	Hammered
3892	Hand In Glove
3893	Hand Off
3894	Hand Over Fist
3895	Hand To Hand Combat
3896	Handle It With Kid Gloves
3897	Hands On
3898	Hands On Approach
3899	Hands On Support
3900	Handwriting Is On The Wall
3901	Handy As A Pocket On A Shirt
3902	Hang Drawn And Quartered
3903	Hang In There
3904	Hang Me Out To Dry
3905	Hang On A Minute
3906	Hang On Every Word
3907	Hang On Tight
3908	Hang Out
3909	Hang Yourself
3910	Hanging By A Moment
3911	Hanging By A Thread
3912	Hanging On By An Eyelash
3913	Happy As A Clam
3914	Happy As A Lark
3915	Happy As A Pig In The Mud

3916	Happy Camper
3917	Happy Days Are Here Again
3918	Happy To Assist
3919	Happy To Help
3920	Happy Trails To You
3921	Hard Days Night
3922	Hard Headed
3923	Hard Hitting Facts
3924	Hard Pill To Swallow
3925	Hard Stop
3926	Hard To Handle
3927	Hard To Swallow
3928	Hardy Har Har
3929	Hare Brained Idea
3930	Harp On
3931	Has A Leg Up
3932	Hasta La Vista Baby
3933	Haste Makes Waste
3934	Hat In Hand
3935	Hat Trick
3936	Hatch An Idea
3937	Hate His Guts
3938	Hate Your Job
3939	Have A Bone To Pick
3940	Have A Bright Future
3941	Have A Change Of Heart
3942	Have A Cow
3943	Have A Field Day
3944	Have A Fling
3945	Have A Heart
3946	Have A Heart Attack
3947	Have A Nice Day
3948	Have A Screw Loose
3949	Have A Shot
3950	Have A Stick Up Your Ass
3951	Have Cold Feet
3952	Have It Your Way
3953	Have No Fear
3954	Have The Goods On Them
3955	Have The Last Laugh

76

3956	Have You Been Drinking The Kool Aid
3957	Have You No Sense Of Decency
3958	Have Your Bell Rung
3959	Have Your Cake And Eat It Too
3960	Have Your Nose In The Air
3961	Have Your Nose Put Out Of Joint
3962	Haven't Got A Penny To My Name
3963	Haven't Got A Row To Hoe
3964	Haven't Seen This In Ages
3965	Having The Time Of My Life
3966	Having To Say You're Sorry Sucks
3967	Hazy Days Of Summer
3968	He Doesn't Know What Time It Is
3969	He Dogged A Bullet
3970	He Got Mugged
3971	He Has Egg On His Face
3972	He Has Great IQ
3973	He Learned His Lesson
3974	He Lost The Handle
3975	He Met His Waterloo
3976	He Never Met A Doughnut He Didn't Like
3977	He Should Have His Head Examined
3978	He Wasn't Man Enough
3979	He Went That A Way
3980	He Who Calls The Tune Must Pay The Piper
3981	He Who Cannot Dance Blames The DJ
3982	He Who Hesitates Is Lost
3983	He Who Laughs Last Laughs Best

3984	He Who Lives By The Sword Shall Die By The Sword
3985	He Who Never Made A Mistake Never Made Anything
3986	He Wouldn't Hurt A Fly
3987	Head And Shoulders Above The Rest
3988	Head Liner
3989	Head Over Heels
3990	Head To Head
3991	Heading For The Poor House
3992	Heads I Win Tails You Lose
3993	Heads Or Tails
3994	Heads Up
3995	Heads Will Roll
3996	Hear Me Out
3997	Hear No Evil See No Evil Speak No Evil
3998	Heard It Through The Grapevine
3999	Heart Breaker
4000	Heart Of Gold
4001	Heart Of Stone
4002	Heart Over Mind
4003	Heart To Heart
4004	Heaven Help Us
4005	Heavens To Betsy
4006	Hedge One's Bets
4007	Heeeere's Johnny
4008	Heh Heh
4009	Heirloom
4010	Hell Bender
4011	Hell Bent For Election
4012	Hell Bent For Leather
4013	Hell Hath No Furry Like A Women Scorned
4014	Hell In A Hand Basket
4015	Hell Of A Ride
4016	Hell On Wheels

4017	Hell Raiser
4018	He'll Set The World On Fire
4019	He'll Try To Sell You The Brooklyn Bridge
4020	Hello Gorgeous
4021	Hells Bells
4022	Hem And Haw
4023	Hen Pecked
4024	Hep Cat
4025	Her Biological Clock Is Ticking
4026	Here Come The Judge
4027	Here Goes
4028	Here Here
4029	Here I Am
4030	Here I Are
4031	Here I Stand I Can Do Other
4032	Here It Is
4033	Here It Is Your Moment Of Zen
4034	Here Kitty Kitty Kitty
4035	Here Today Gone Tomorrow
4036	Here We Go
4037	Here We Go Again
4038	Here's A Good Bet
4039	Here's Johnny
4040	Here's Looking At You Kid
4041	Here's Mud In Your Eye
4042	Here's The Catch
4043	Here's The Deal
4044	Here's The Keys To Fort Knox
4045	Here's The Kicker
4046	Here's The Rub
4047	Here's Your Hat What's Your Hurry
4048	He's Clutch
4049	He's Got A Bug Up His Ass
4050	He's Got Game
4051	He's Got More Money Than He Knows What To Do With

4052	He's Got The Skills To Pay The Bills
4053	He's Hot
4054	He's Milk Toast
4055	He's Money
4056	He's The Big Cheese
4057	He's Toast
4058	Hey Good Lookin' What You Got Cookin'
4059	Hey Hey Hey
4060	Hey Kids What Time Is It
4061	Hey Man What's Up
4062	Hey That's Unfair
4063	Hey Zipperhead
4064	Hi Curly Kill Anyone Today
4065	Hi Jack
4066	Hi Oh Silver
4067	Hickory Dickory Dock
4068	Hide The Salami
4069	Hide Your Light Under A Bushel
4070	High And Tight
4071	High As A Kite
4072	High Ball
4073	High Falutin
4074	High Hopes
4075	High Jinks
4076	High Maintenance
4077	High Muck
4078	High Muckety Mucks
4079	High On The Hog
4080	High Seas
4081	Highway Robbery
4082	Hill Billy
4083	Hindsight Is Twenty-Twenty
4084	Hip Hip Hooray
4085	His Bark Is Worse Than His Bite
4086	His Clutch
4087	His Elevator Doesn't Go To The Top Floor

4088	His Eyes Are Bigger Than His Stomach
4089	His Left Hand Doesn't Know What His Right Hand Is Doing
4090	His Money Isn't Any Good Here
4091	His Mouth Is Writing Checks His Body Can't Cash
4092	History In The Making
4093	History Repeats Itself
4094	Hit Below The Belt
4095	Hit 'Em In The Head With A Wood Stick Stanley
4096	Hit 'Em Up With Style
4097	Hit Every Ugly Branch Falling Out Of The Tree
4098	Hit Him Right Between The Numbers
4099	Hit Me With Your Best Shot
4100	Hit On
4101	Hit Pay Dirt
4102	Hit Rock Bottom
4103	Hit The Books
4104	Hit The Bricks
4105	Hit The Deck
4106	Hit The Hay
4107	Hit The Nail On The Head
4108	Hit The Road
4109	Hit The Sack
4110	Hitch Hike
4111	Hitch Your Wagon To A Star
4112	Hitting Below The Belt
4113	Hitting On All Six
4114	Hob Gobblin
4115	Hob Nob
4116	Hocus Pocus
4117	Hodge Podge
4118	Hoe Your Own Row
4119	Hog Heaven Be In

4120	Hog Wash
4121	Hogs Head
4122	Hoist Your Own Flag
4123	Hoity Toity
4124	Hold A Candle To
4125	Hold At Bay
4126	Hold The Phone
4127	Hold The Presses
4128	Hold Your Breath Till You Turn Blue
4129	Hold Your Head Up
4130	Hold Your Horses
4131	Holding All The Cards
4132	Holding Down The Fort
4133	Holding The Bag
4134	Holding The Wrong End Of The Stick
4135	Holding Your Feet To The Fire
4136	Holy Cow
4137	Holy Crap
4138	Holy Mackerel
4139	Holy Smokes
4140	Home Away From Home
4141	Home Is Where The Heart Is
4142	Home Is Where You Hang Your Hat
4143	Home Run King
4144	Home Sweet Home
4145	Honest To Goodness
4146	Honesty Is The Best Policy
4147	Honey Catches More Flies Than Vinegar
4148	Honey Don't Play That
4149	Honey I'm Home
4150	Honey Moon
4151	Honky Tonk
4152	Honor Thy Father And Thy Mother
4153	Hood Winked
4154	Hook And Book

79

4155	Hook Line And Sinker	4189	How About A Little Respect
4156	Hook Me Up	4190	How Come
4157	Hooray For Hollywood	4191	How Do I Love The Let Me Count The Ways
4158	Hoot Nanny		
4159	Hop Skip And A Jump	4192	How Do You Do
4160	Hope Against Hope	4193	How Do You Like Them Apples
4161	Hope Chest		
4162	Hope For The Best Prepare For The Worst	4194	How Does That Grab You
		4195	How It Works
4163	Hope Springs Eternal	4196	How It's Going
4164	Hope That Helps	4197	How Long Has This Been Going On
4165	Horn Swoggle		
4166	Horny As A Peach Orchard Boar	4198	How Much Is That Doggie In The Window
		4199	How Much Wood Can A Woodchuck Chuck
4167	Horny As A Three Peckered Billy Goat		
		4200	How Sweet It Is
4168	Horse Apiece	4201	How Time Flies
4169	Horse Around	4202	How You Doin'
4170	Horse Of A Different Color	4203	How'd You Like To Get A Fat Lip
4171	Horse Sense		
4172	Horseshoe Up His Butt	4204	Howdy Doody
4173	Horsing Around	4205	Howl At The Moon
4174	Hot As Hell	4206	How's It Hanging
4175	Hot Beef Injection	4207	How's That For A Topper
4176	Hot Dog	4208	How's This For A Turn Of Events
4177	Hot Enough For You		
4178	Hot Enough To Fry An Egg	4209	Hub Bub
4179	Hot Hand	4210	Hum Bug
4180	Hot Headed	4211	Hum Drum
4181	Hot Hot Hot	4212	Human Nature Doesn't Change
4182	Hot Off The Press		
4183	Hot On The Trail	4213	Hump Day
4184	Hot Rods And Muscle Cars	4214	Humpty Dumpty Sat On A Wall
4185	Hotter Than A Fox In A Firestorm		
		4215	Hung By Your Own Petard
4186	Hotter Than Georgia Asphalt	4216	Hunker Down
		4217	Hunky Dory
4187	House Divided Against Itself Cannot Stand	4218	Hunt And Peck
		4219	Hurl Insults
4188	Houston We Have A Problem	4220	Hurly Burly

80

4221	Hurry Before The Price Increases
4222	Hurry Scurry
4223	Hurts Like The Dickens
4224	Hush Puppy
4225	I Absolutely Refuse To Be Assertive
4226	I Am Big It's The Pictures That Got Small
4227	I Am Bored
4228	I Am My Brothers Keeper
4229	I Am Myself And I'm Going To Continue To Play That Role
4230	I Am Not A Crook
4231	I Am Not Growing Like A Weed
4232	I Am Serious And Don't Call Me Shirley
4233	I Am The Va-Va-Voom Girl
4234	I Am Wankered
4235	I Am What I Am That's What I Am
4236	I Assure You
4237	I Became Insane With Long Intervals Of Horrible Sanity
4238	I Beg To Differ
4239	I Bought It For A Song
4240	I Busted My Hump
4241	I Came I Saw I Conquered
4242	I Can Do That
4243	I Can Only Ignore One Thing At A Time
4244	I Can See The Carrot At The End Of The Tunnel
4245	I Can't Deny It
4246	I Cannot Tell A Lie
4247	I Can't Believe I Ate The Whole Thing
4248	I Can't Stand It
4249	I Can't Stand People Who Look Down On People
4250	I Can't Stomach That
4251	I Can't Stop Loving You
4252	I Can't Tell You What A Pleasure Its Been
4253	I Can't Think When I Concentrate
4254	I Come In Peace
4255	I Could Eat A Horse
4256	I Could Whip You With One Arm Tied Behind My Back
4257	I Could Write A Book
4258	I Coulda Been A Contender
4259	I Coulda Been Somebody
4260	I Couldn't Agree More
4261	I Couldn't Agree With You More
4262	I Couldn't Believe My Eyes
4263	I Couldn't Care Less
4264	I Count The Minutes
4265	I Didn't Come Down The Clyde In A Banana Boat
4266	I Didn't Do It
4267	I Didn't Expect The Spanish Inquisition
4268	I Didn't Have Sexual Relations With That Woman
4269	I Didn't Know My Own Strength
4270	I Didn't Know The Gun Was Loaded
4271	I Don't Believe You
4272	I Don't Want To Miss A Thing
4273	I Don't Give A Damn
4274	I Don't Know Where To Begin
4275	I Don't Want To Hear A Peep Out Of You
4276	I Enjoy Your Company Most When I Am By Myself

4277	I Feel A Lot More Like I Do Now Than I Did When I Came In
4278	I Feel Into The Same Trap
4279	I Feel The Need The Need For Speed
4280	I Feel Your Pain
4281	I Get A Kick From Champaign
4282	I Get A Kick Out Of You
4283	I Get Excited
4284	I Get No Respect
4285	I Got A Feeling
4286	I Got Hosed
4287	I Guess That's Why They Call It The Blues
4288	I Hate To Say This But
4289	I Have A Bone To Pick With You
4290	I Have A Dream
4291	I Have An Ax To Grind
4292	I Have Miles To Go Before I Sleep
4293	I Have News For You
4294	I Have No Bones About That
4295	I Have Not Yet Begun To Fight
4296	I Have Seen The Future And It Works
4297	I Have Something To Say But I Don't Know What
4298	I Haven't A Clue
4299	I Haven't The Foggiest
4300	I Hear You Knocking
4301	I Hear You Loud And Clear
4302	I Hear You're Mother Calling
4303	I Heard That
4304	I Heard It Through The Grapevine
4305	I Heard That

4306	I Honestly Love You
4307	I Just Couldn't Help Myself
4308	I Just Did The Unthinkable
4309	I Just Flipped
4310	I Just Had To Get This Off My Chest
4311	I Just Want To Celebrate
4312	I Know Kung Fu
4313	I Know Nothing
4314	I Left My Heart In San Francisco
4315	I Like It Rough
4316	I Like You So Much Better When You're Naked
4317	I Love It When A Plan Come Together
4318	I Love The Smell Of Napalm In The Morning
4319	I Love You
4320	I Must Be Seeing Things
4321	I Need It Yesterday
4322	I Need That Like A Hole In The Head
4323	I Need That Like A Moose Needs A Hat Rack
4324	I Need That Like I Need A Hole In My Head
4325	I Need To Know
4326	I Never Have Enough Time
4327	I Never Met A Man I Didn't Like
4328	I Never Met A Woman I Didn't Like
4329	I Never Thought It Could Happen To Me
4330	I Only Have Eyes For You
4331	I Only Have Two Hands
4332	I Only Regret That I Have But One Life To Give
4333	I Ought To Tan Your Hide

4334	I Predict
4335	I Put Two And Two Together
4336	I Quit Smoking Cold Turkey
4337	I Really Don't Want To Know
4338	I Saw The Light
4339	I Second That
4340	I See Dead People
4341	I Shall Return
4342	I Should Have Done Something
4343	I Should Have Known Better
4344	I Should Have Seen It Coming
4345	I Smell A Rat
4346	I Started To Work My Mojo
4347	I Think I Love You
4348	I Think That I Shall Never See A Poem Lovely As A Tree
4349	I Think Therefore I Am
4350	I Told You So
4351	I Trust Him As Far As I Can Throw Him
4352	I Want My MTV
4353	I Want My Place In The Sun
4354	I Want To Be Alone
4355	I Want To Hear The Voice Of The Great Silent Majority
4356	I Want To Thank My Lord And Savior
4357	I Warned You
4358	I Was Not Born Yesterday
4359	I Was Roped Into It
4360	I Wasn't Born Yesterday
4361	I Will Defend To The Death Your Right To Say It
4362	I Will Survive
4363	I Wish I Knew How To Quit You

4364	I Wonder
4365	I Won't Take No For An Answer
4366	I Work Night And Day
4367	I Would Not Count Them Out
4368	I Wouldn't Give Him The Time Of Day
4369	I Wouldn't Piss On Your Teeth If They Were On Fire
4370	I Wouldn't Touch It With A Ten Foot Pole
4371	I Wouldn't Trust Him As Far As I Could Spit
4372	I Wouldn't Want To Be In His Shoes
4373	I Wouldn't Want To Meet Him In A Dark Alley
4374	I'll Never Stop
4375	Ice Water In His Veins
4376	Icing On The Cake
4377	I'd Bet My Bottom Dollar
4378	I'd Give My Right Arm To Be Ambidextrous
4379	I'd Lose My Head If It Wasn't Attached
4380	I'd Rather Be A Hammer Than A Nail
4381	I'd Rather Die On My Feet Than Live On My Knees
4382	Idle Chit Chat
4383	Idle Hands Are The Devil's Tools
4384	Idle Hands Are The Devil's Workshop
4385	If A Frog Had Wings He Wouldn't Bump His Ass Hoppin'
4386	If A Pig Had Wings It Could Fly
4387	If A Tree Falls In The Forest Does It Make A Sound

83

4388	If Anything Can Go Wrong It Will	4408	If It's Worth Doing It's Worth Doing Well
4389	If At First You Don't Succeed Try Try Again	4409	If I've Said It Once I've Said It A Thousand Times
4390	If Everything Goes Perfectly Something's Wrong	4410	If Looks Could Kill
4391	If God Had Meant For Man To Fly He Would've Given Us Wings	4411	If Not Us Who If Not Now When
4392	If He Were Alive Today He'd Turn Over In His Grave	4412	If The Mountain Won't Come To Mohammed Mohammed Must Go To The Mountain
4393	If His Word Were A Bridge You'd Be Afraid To Cross	4413	If The Shoe Fits Wear It
4394	If I Had A Dime For Every	4414	If There's Anything I Can't Stand It's Intolerance
4395	If I Had A Nickel For Every Time That Happened I'd Be A Millionaire	4415	If We Don't Hang Together We'll Hang Separately
		4416	If Wishes Were Horse Beggars Will Ride
4396	If I Had Known How Successful I Was Going To Be I Wouldn't Have Worked So Hard	4417	If Wishes Were Horses Beggars Would Ride
		4418	If You Believe That I've Got A Bridge To Sell You
4397	If I Told You Once I've Told You A Thousand Times	4419	If You Build It They Will Come
4398	If I Were A Rich Man	4420	If You Can Make It Here You Can Make It Anywhere
4399	If I Were In His Shoes	4421	If You Can't Beat 'Em Join 'Em
4400	If I'm Not Back In Five Minutes Wait Longer	4422	If You Can't Beat Them Arrange To Have Them Beaten
4401	If It Ain't Broke Don't Fix It	4423	If You Can't Beat Them Join Them
4402	If It Doesn't Fit You Must Acquit	4424	If You Can't Find It Grind It
4403	If It Doesn't Pan Out	4425	If You Can't Kill The King Then Don't Wound Him
4404	If It Looks Like A Duck		
4405	If It Weren't For Bad Luck I'd Have No Luck At All	4426	If You Can't Run With The Big Dogs Stay Under The Porch
4406	If It Weren't For You Meddling Kids	4427	If You Can't See The Bottom Don't Put Your Foot In The Water
4407	If It's Not One Thing It's Another		

4428	If You Can't Stand The Heat Get Out Of The Kitchen	4448	If You've Seen One You've Seen Them All
4429	If You Chase Two Rabbits Both Will Escape	4449	Ignorance Is Bliss
4430	If You Could Read My Mind	4450	Ignorance Of The Law Is No Excuse
4431	If You Don't Have Anything Nice To Say Don't Say Anything At All	4451	I'll Be A Monkey's Uncle
		4452	I'll Be A Son Of A Gun
4432	If You Don't Like It Lump It	4453	I'll Be Back
4433	If You Get The Sense And Chuck The Tense	4454	I'll Be Back In Two Shakes Of A Lamb's Tail
4434	If You Know What I Mean	4455	I'll Be Damned
4435	If You Love Something Set It Free	4456	I'll Be Quick
4436	If You Play Your Cards Right	4457	I'll Be The Judge Of That Thank You
4437	If You Think About It Long Enough You'll See That It's Obvious	4458	I'll Bet Dollars To Doughnuts
		4459	I'll Do Whatever It takes
		4460	Ill Fated Idea
4438	If You Want Peace Prepare For War	4461	I'll Fix You
4439	If You Want Something Done Right Do It Yourself	4462	I'll Fix Your Little Red Wagon
		4463	I'll Get You My Pretty
4440	If You Were Any Closer It Would Bite You	4464	I'll Get You My Pretty And Your Little Dog Too
4441	If You Won't Pull It Together For Yourself No One Else Will	4465	I'll Have What She's Having
		4466	I'll Knock You Into Next Week
4442	If Your Foresight Was As Good As Your Hindsight We Would Be Better By A Far Sight	4467	I'll Leave You With Something To Chew On
		4468	I'll Pay You
		4469	I'll Procrastinate Later
4443	If You're Going To Talk The Talk You Better Walk The Walk	4470	I'll Punch His Lights Out
		4471	I'll See You In Hell
		4472	I'll See You Tomorrow
4444	If You're In A Hurry Time Flies	4473	I'll Show You
4445	If You're Not Part Of The Solution You're Part Of The Problem	4474	I'll Teach You Anything Just Don't Eat Me
		4475	I'm A Believer
		4476	I'm All Ears
4446	If You're Serious	4477	I'm All Thumbs
4447	If You've Got It Flaunt It	4478	I'm An Atheist Thank God

85

4479	I'm Back In The Saddle Again
4480	I'm Certain But I Could Be Wrong
4481	I'm Feeling Lucky
4482	I'm From Missouri You've Got To Show Me
4483	I'm Going Bananas
4484	I'm Going To Be Healthy If It Kills Me
4485	I'm Going To Make Him An Offer You Can't Refuse
4486	I'm Going To Tell Your Mother
4487	I'm Gonna Clean Your Clock
4488	I'm Gonna Lay Down The Law
4489	I'm Gonna Wash That Man Right Outta My Hair
4490	I'm Having A Really Bad Hair Day
4491	I'm In A Pickle Now
4492	I'm In Hog Heaven
4493	I'm Just Big Boned
4494	I'm Larry This Is My Brother Darryl
4495	I'm Lost For Words
4496	I'm Mad As Hell
4497	I'm Not A Crook
4498	I'm Not A Doctor But I Play One On TV
4499	I'm Not A Rocket Scientist
4500	I'm Not Getting Any Younger
4501	I'm Not Kidding
4502	I'm Old Fashioned
4503	I'm On A Roll
4504	I'm Only Flesh And Blood
4505	I'm Outta Here
4506	I'm Racking My Brains
4507	I'm Ready

4508	I'm Ready For My Close Up
4509	I'm Soooo Excited
4510	I'm Speaking From Experience
4511	I'm Telling Your Mother
4512	I'm The King Of The World
4513	I'm The Lowest On The Pecking Pole
4514	I'm The Man
4515	I'm Throwing In The Towel
4516	I'm Walking Here I'm Walking Here
4517	I'm Working For A Living
4518	Imagine The Possibilities
4519	Imitation Is The Sincerest Form Of Flattery
4520	Improve Your Aim
4521	Improve Your Life
4522	In A Blue Funk
4523	In A Blue Moon
4524	In A Class All By Itself
4525	In A Coon's Age
4526	In A Coon's Age Not To Have Seen Someone
4527	In A Flash
4528	In A Funk
4529	In A Hole
4530	In A Jam
4531	In A New York Minute
4532	In A Nutshell
4533	In A Pickle
4534	In A Pig's Eye
4535	In A Pinch
4536	In A Rush
4537	In A Wink
4538	In Apple Pie Order
4539	In Bed With One's Boots On
4540	In Cahoots With
4541	In Cold Blood
4542	In Defeat Defiance

86

4543	In Every Life A Little Rain Must Fall	4577	In The Buff
4544	In Fine Fettle	4578	In The Clear
4545	In For A Fleecing	4579	In The Clouds
4546	In For A Long Cold Winter	4580	In The Doghouse
4547	In For A Penny In For A Pound	4581	In The Doldrums
4548	In For The Long Haul	4582	In The Dumps
4549	In Full Cry	4583	In The End
4550	In God We Trust	4584	In The Eye Of The Tiger
4551	In Good Company	4585	In The Groove
4552	In Harm's Way	4586	In The Hot Seat
4553	In Hog Heaven	4587	In The House
4554	In Hot Water	4588	In The Joint
4555	In My Opinion	4589	In The Lap Of Luxury
4556	In No Time	4590	In The Limelight
4557	In On The Ground Floor	4591	In The Money
4558	In One Ear And Out The Other	4592	In The Nick Of Time
4559	In One Fell Swoop	4593	In The Palm Of Your Hand
4560	In Only 30 Minutes	4594	In The Pink
4561	In Only Seconds	4595	In The Pod
4562	In Other Words	4596	In The Red
4563	In Our Neck Of The Woods	4597	In The Right Place At The Right Time
4564	In Over Your Head	4598	In The Same Boat
4565	In Peace Good Will	4599	In The Wild
4566	In Real Time	4600	In The Zone
4567	In Seventh Heaven	4601	In Two Shakes Of A Lamb's Tail
4568	In Spring A Young Man's Fancy Turns To Love	4602	In Unity There Is Strength
4569	In Still Weather Everyone Is A Good Sailor	4603	In Victory Magnanimity
		4604	In War Resolution
4570	In Terms Of The Richter Scale This Defeat Was A Force Eight Gale	4605	In War There Is No Substitute For Victory
		4606	In Wine There's Truth
4571	In The 1st Degree	4607	In Your Dreams
4572	In The Bag	4608	In Your Face
4573	In The Beginning	4609	Inched Out
4574	In The Black	4610	Include Me Out
4575	In The Black Be	4611	Include The Kitchen Sink
4576	In The Blink Of An Eye	4612	Incredible Odds
		4613	Independent As A Hog On Ice

4614	Indian Giver
4615	Innocent As The Day He Was Born
4616	Innocent Until Proven Guilty
4617	Iron Curtain
4618	Is A Frog's Ass Water Tight
4619	Is A Pig Pork
4620	Is It Safe
4621	Is It Soup Yet
4622	Is Nothing Sacred
4623	Is That A Gun In Your Pocket Or Are You Just Happy To See Me
4624	Is That Your Final Answer
4625	Is The Glass Half Empty Or Half Full
4626	Is The Pope Catholic
4627	Is This Heaven
4628	Ish Kabibble
4629	Isn't All It's Cracked Up To Be
4630	Isn't It A Small World
4631	Isn't That Special
4632	It Ain't Over Until It's Over
4633	It Ain't Rocket Science
4634	It All Boils Down To This
4635	It All Comes Out In The Wash
4636	It Comes With The Territory
4637	It Could Happen To You
4638	It Doesn't Get Any Better Than This
4639	It Feels So Good
4640	It Figures
4641	It Goes Against The Grain
4642	It Goes In One Ear And Out The Other
4643	It Had To Be You
4644	It Is Better To Lose The Battle And Win The War
4645	It Is Good To Be King

4646	It Is More Devine To Give Than Receive
4647	It Isn't All Sweetness And Light
4648	It Just Goes To Show
4649	It Just Hit Me Like A Ton Of Bricks
4650	It Keeps Going Going And Going
4651	It Matters To Me
4652	It Must've Been Love
4653	It Never Rains But It Pours
4654	It Runs In The Family
4655	It Seems Like Only Yesterday
4656	It Stands To Reason
4657	It Suits You To A "T"
4658	It Take Two To Make A Quarrel
4659	It Takes A Heap Of Living To Make A House A Home
4660	It Takes A Licking
4661	It Takes A Thief To Catch A Thief
4662	It Takes A Village To Raise A Child
4663	It Takes One To Know One
4664	It Takes Two To Tango
4665	It Takes Two Wings To Fly
4666	It Took My Breath Away
4667	It Was A Piece Of Cake
4668	It Was A White Knuckle Ride
4669	It Was An Ill Fated Idea
4670	It Was Beauty That Killed The Beast
4671	It Was That Game That Put The Ship Back On The Road
4672	It Was The Best Of Times It Was The Worst Of Times
4673	It Was Worth It

4674	It Will All Come Out In The Wash
4675	It Will Be A Cold Day In Hell
4676	It Will Do
4677	It Will Play In Peoria
4678	It Won't Fly
4679	It Won't Wash
4680	It Works For Me
4681	It's All In The Game
4682	It's Been Awhile
4683	It's My Life
4684	It's My Party
4685	It's Now Or Never
4686	It's Only Make Believe
4687	It's Still Rock N Roll To Me
4688	Itching Palms
4689	It'll Change The Way You Look At Things
4690	It'll Never Fly
4691	It's A Barn Burner
4692	It's A Catch 22
4693	It's A Cinch
4694	It's A Close Call
4695	It's A Crap Shoot
4696	It's A Crying Shame
4697	It's A Dirty Job But Somebody's Got To Do It
4698	It's A Dog Eat Dog World
4699	Its A Dog's Life
4700	It's A Dream Come True
4701	It's A Drop In The Bucket
4702	It's A Fact
4703	It's A Family Tradition
4704	It's A Freckle Past A Hair
4705	It's A Game Of Inches
4706	It's A Grist For The Mill
4707	It's A Jungle Out There
4708	It's A Labor Of Love
4709	It's A Lemon
4710	It's A Long Shot
4711	It's A Matter Of Trust

4712	It's A New Day
4713	It's A No Go
4714	It's A One Horse Town
4715	It's A Piece Of Cake
4716	It's A Route I've Considered
4717	It's A Shoe In
4718	It's A Sign Of The Times
4719	It's A Small World
4720	It's A Snap
4721	Its A Sure Thing
4722	It's A Wash
4723	It's A Wonderful Life
4724	It's A Zoo Out There
4725	It's Ain't Nothing
4726	It's Alive It's Alive
4727	Its All Cut And Dried
4728	It's All Fun And Games Until Someone Loses An Eye
4729	Its All Greek To Me
4730	It's All In A Day's Work
4731	It's All In The Family
4732	It's All In Your Head
4733	It's All Over And Done With
4734	It's All Over But The Crying
4735	It's All Over But The Shouting
4736	It's All Over Town
4737	It's All Part Of The Job
4738	It's All Smoke And Mirrors
4739	It's All Systems Go
4740	Its All Topsy Turvy
4741	It's Almost Like Taking Candy From A Baby
4742	It's Always Darkest Just Before Dawn
4743	It's Always Possible
4744	It's An 800 Pound Gorilla
4745	It's An Albatross Around Your Neck

89

4746	It's An Ill Wind That Blows No Good
4747	It's As Easy As Leading Fish To Water
4748	It's Autumn In Her Mouth And All Her Tongue Can Do Is Rustle
4749	It's Best To Act Now
4750	It's Better Than A Poke In The Eye With A Sharp Stick
4751	It's Better Than A Sharp Stick In The Eye
4752	It's Better To Be A Big Fish In A Little Pond
4753	It's Better To Be Happy Than Wise
4754	It's Better To Be Killed Than Frightened To Death
4755	It's Better To Be On The Safe Side
4756	It's Better To Light A Candle Than To Curse The Darkness
4757	It's Better To Travel Hopefully Than To Arrive
4758	It's Business As Usual
4759	It's Cutting Edge
4760	It's Darkest Just Before The Dawn
4761	It's Déjà Vu All Over Again
4762	It's Easier For A Camel To Pass Through The Eye Of A Needle
4763	It's Easy For You To Say
4764	It's Easy To Be Wise After The Event
4765	It's Getting Out Of Hand
4766	It's Gonna Get Better
4767	It's Got A Great Beat But You Can't Dance To It
4768	It's Greek To Me
4769	It's In Our Baby Boomer

	DNA
4770	It's In The Bag
4771	It's In The Blood
4772	It's In The Cards
4773	It's In The Lap Of The Gods
4774	It's Just One Of Those Days I Guess
4775	It's Just What The Doctor Ordered
4776	It's Kind Of Fun To Do The Impossible
4777	Its Like My Daddy Used To Say
4778	It's Like Riding A Bicycle
4779	It's Like Taking Candy From A Baby
4780	It's Love That Make The World Go Round
4781	It's Music To My Ears
4782	It's Neck And Neck
4783	It's Never Too Late To Learn
4784	It's No Skin Off My Nose
4785	It's No Use Crying Over Spilled Milk
4786	It's None Of Your Business
4787	It's Not A Sprint It's A Marathon
4788	It's Not All It's Cracked Up To Be
4789	It's Not My Cup Of Tea
4790	It's Not Over Till It's Over
4791	It's Not The End Of The World
4792	It's Not The Heat It's The Humidity
4793	It's Not The Size Of The Dog In The Fight It's The Size Of The Fight In The Dog
4794	It's Not Too Late For Your Spring Cleaning

90

4795	It's Not What You Know It's Who You Know
4796	It's Not What You Say But How You Say It
4797	It's Not Whether You Win Or Lose It's How You Play The Game
4798	It's Not Worth The Paper It's Written On
4799	It's Not Written In Stone
4800	It's Nothing Earth Shattering
4801	It's Now Or Never
4802	It's On The Tip On My Tongue
4803	It's One Of A Kind
4804	It's Only A Matter Of Time
4805	It's Only Business
4806	It's Out Of My Hands
4807	It's Out Of This World
4808	It's Politics As Usual
4809	It's Probably A Lot Worse Than It Is
4810	It's Raining Like A Cow Pissing On A Flat Rock
4811	It's Right Under Your Nose In Plain Sight
4812	It's Showtime
4813	It's So Easy
4814	It's Takes All Kinds Of People
4815	It's The Bomb
4816	It's The Cards
4817	It's The Economy Stupid
4818	It's The First Step That Costs
4819	It's The Only Game In Town
4820	It's The Real McCoy
4821	It's The Real Thing
4822	It's The Thought That Counts
4823	It's The Tip Of The Iceberg

4824	It's Time For A Change
4825	It's Time To Grow Up
4826	It's Time To Set The Record Straight
4827	It's Too Good To Be True
4828	It's Too Little Too Late
4829	It's Too Much Of A Good Thing
4830	It's What's On The Inside That Counts
4831	It's Written In The Stars
4832	It's Your Funeral
4833	It'sTurkey Time
4834	I've Been Had
4835	I've Got A Monkey On My Back
4836	I've Got A Tiger By The Tail
4837	I've Got A Winner
4838	I've Got It Covered
4839	I've Got Other Fish To Fry
4840	I've Got You Over A Barrel
4841	I've Gotta Be Me
4842	I've Had It Up To Here
4843	I've Heard That Before
4844	I've Said It Before And I'll Say It Again
4845	I've Told You A Million Times Not To Exaggerate
4846	Ivy League
4847	Jack Knife
4848	Jack Of All Trades And A Master Of None
4849	Jane You Ignorant Slut
4850	Jerk Off
4851	Jerk Water
4852	Jig Is Up
4853	Jiggle Your Bait
4854	Jim Dandy To The Rescue
4855	Jiminy Christmas
4856	Jingle Bells
4857	Jockeying For Position

91

4858	Joe Doe Investigation	4890	Just Give Me One Good Reason
4859	Johnny Come Lately		
4860	Join The Ranks	4891	Just In The Nick Of Time
4861	Joined At The Hip	4892	Just In Time
4862	Joined At The Hip Be	4893	Just Kidding
4863	Jokers Wild	4894	Just Like Magic
4864	Journey Back Into The Past	4895	Just Like Riding A Bike
4865	Journey Of A Thousand Miles Begins With The First Step	4896	Just Once
		4897	Just One More Thing
		4898	Just One Of Those Things
4866	Judge Not According To Appearances	4899	Just Press The Easy Button
4867	Judge Not That Ye Be Not Judged	4900	Just Put Your Lips Together And Blow
4868	Jump Down Your Throat	4901	Just Requires Lots Of Hard Work
4869	Jump In With Both Feet		
4870	Jump On The Bandwagon	4902	Just Say No
4871	Jump Over The Broomstick	4903	Just The Ticket
4872	Jump The Gun	4904	Just The Tip Of The Iceberg
4873	Jump Through The Hoops	4905	Just Thought I'd Throw That In
4874	Jumped Her/His Bones		
4875	Jumping Off Place	4906	Just Under The Wire
4876	Jury Is Still Out	4907	Just Washed My Hair And Cant Do A Thing With It
4877	Jury Is Still Out The		
4878	Just A Cotton Pickin' Minute Here	4908	Just What The Doctor Ordered
4879	Just A Drop In The Bucket	4909	Just When You Think You've Seen It All
4880	Just A Minute		
4881	Just A Second	4910	Just Wing It
4882	Just Admiring The View	4911	Justice Is Blind
4883	Just Around The Bend	4912	Kangaroo Court
4884	Just As Sweet As You Please	4913	Kangaroo Loose In The Top Paddock
4885	Just Because I Have Nothing To Say Is No Reason Not To Listen To Me	4914	Keep A Bad Dog With You And The Good Dogs Won't Bite
		4915	Keep A Stiff Upper Lip
4886	Just Breathe	4916	Keep 'Em Flying
4887	Just Duckie	4917	Keep Hope Alive
4888	Just Fell Off The Turnip Truck	4918	Keep In Touch
		4919	Keep It Down
4889	Just For The Hell Of It	4920	Keep It On The Table

92

4921	Keep It Simple Stupid
4922	Keep It Under Your Hat
4923	Keep My Eye On You
4924	Keep On Your Toes
4925	Keep Something At Bay
4926	Keep The Ball Rolling
4927	Keep The Home Fires Burning
4928	Keep The Light On
4929	Keep The Pot Boiling
4930	Keep The Wolf From The Door
4931	Keep You Finger's Crossed
4932	Keep Your Chin Up
4933	Keep Your Eye On The Ball
4934	Keep Your Eye On The Prize
4935	Keep Your Eyes Open
4936	Keep Your Eyes Open And Your Mouth Shut
4937	Keep Your Eyes Peeled
4938	Keep Your Feet On The Ground
4939	Keep Your Fingers Crossed
4940	Keep Your Friends Close But Your Enemies Closer
4941	Keep Your Hair On
4942	Keep Your Hands Off
4943	Keep Your Head Down
4944	Keep Your Head In The Game
4945	Keep Your Head On
4946	Keep Your Nose Clean
4947	Keep Your Nose To The Grindstone
4948	Keep Your Pants On
4949	Keep Your Powder Dry
4950	Keep Your Shirt On
4951	Keep Your Shoulder To The Wheel
4952	Keep Your Spirits Up
4953	Keep Your Thing In Your Pants
4954	Keep Your Thoughts To Yourself
4955	Keeper Of The Stars
4956	Keeping An Eye On You
4957	Keeping The World Safe For Democracy
4958	Keeping Time
4959	Keeping Up With The Joneses
4960	Keeps Getting Bette
4961	Keeps Her Cards Close To Her Chest
4962	Keeps His Cards Close To His Vest
4963	Keeps On Ticking
4964	Kettle Of Fish
4965	Kick Back
4966	Kick 'Em When They're Down
4967	Kick 'Em When They're Up And Kick Them When They're Down
4968	Kick Him To The Curb
4969	Kick It
4970	Kick It Up A Notch
4971	Kick Some Butt
4972	Kick The Bucket
4973	Kick To It
4974	Kick Your Feet Up
4975	Kick Your Heels
4976	Kid In A Candy Store
4977	Kids Will Be Kids
4978	Kill All Your Birds With One Stone
4979	Kill 'Em With Kindness I Always Say
4980	Kill The Fatted Cow
4981	Kilroy Was Here
4982	King Of The Blues

4983	King Of The Hill	5019	Know Which Side Your Bread Is Buttered On
4984	King Of The Road		
4985	King's Ransom	5020	Know Your Enemies
4986	Kiss And Make It Better	5021	Knowledge Is Power
4987	Kiss And Make Up	5022	Knows It Chapter And Verse
4988	Kiss And Makeup		
4989	Kiss And Tell	5023	Knuckle Down
4990	Kiss Ass	5024	Knuckle Duster
4991	Kiss My Ass	5025	Knuckle Sandwich
4992	Kiss Of Death	5026	Knuckle Under
4993	Kissing The Rose	5027	Kodak Moment
4994	Kitten On The Keys	5028	La De Dah
4995	Knee High To A Grasshopper	5029	La Dee Da La Dee Da
		5030	Lame Duck
4996	Knickerbockers	5031	Land Lubber
4997	Knife Through Hot Butter	5032	Land Of Milk And Honey
4998	Knock And It Shall Be Opened Unto You	5033	Land Of Nod
		5034	Land Of Oz
4999	Knock 'Em Dead	5035	Land Of The Free And Home Of The Brave
5000	Knock It Off		
5001	Knock It Out Of The Park	5036	Land Of The Mohicans
5002	Knock Off	5037	Larger Than Life
5003	Knock On Wood	5038	Larger Than Life Itself
5004	Knock The Cover Off The Ball	5039	Last But Not Least
		5040	Last Ditch Effort
5005	Knock The Spots Off Of You	5041	Last Gasp
		5042	Last Hurrah
5006	Knock The Tar Out Of You	5043	Last One In Is A Rotten Egg
5007	Knock Your Socks Off	5044	Last Straw That Breaks The Camel's Back
5008	Knock Yourself Out		
5009	Knocked Me Off My Feet	5045	Laugh A Minute
5010	Knocked Up	5046	Laugh And The World Laughs With You
5011	Knockin' On Heaven's Door		
5012	Knockout	5047	Laughing All The Way To The Bank
5013	Knockout Blow		
5014	Know It Like The Back Of My Hand	5048	Laughter Is Still The Best Medicine
5015	Know The Ropes	5049	Lay An Egg
5016	Know The Score	5050	Lay Down The Law
5017	Know What's Up	5051	Lay It On The Line
5018	Know Where You Stand	5052	Lay My Cards On The Table

94

5053	Lay My Cards All Out On The Table In Front Of You
5054	Lazy Susan
5055	Lead By The Nose
5056	Leader Of The Pack
5057	Lean And Mean
5058	Leap Frog
5059	Leap In The Dark
5060	Learn From The Mistakes Of Others
5061	Learning Curve
5062	Learning To Live Again
5063	Learning Without Thinking Is A Dangerous Thing
5064	Least Said Soonest Mended
5065	Leather Neck
5066	Leave In The Lurch
5067	Leave No Stone Unturned
5068	Leave Well Enough Alone
5069	Leave Your Mark
5070	Leaves No Stone Unturned
5071	Left At The Altar
5072	Left Handed Compliment
5073	Left Holding The Bag
5074	Left In The Lurch
5075	Left It On The Table
5076	Left Leaving With Your Tail Between Your Legs
5077	Left Me Gasping For Breath
5078	Left Scraping The Bottom Of The Barrel
5079	Legend In His Own Mind
5080	Lend Me Your Ears
5081	Leopard Can't Change It's Spots
5082	Le's Get The Party Started
5083	Less Is More
5084	Lesser Of Two Evils
5085	Lest We Forget
5086	Let Bygones Be Bygones

5087	Let 'Er Rip
5088	Let God Sort 'Em Out
5089	Let Him Without Sin Cast The First Stone
5090	Let It Be
5091	Let It Grow
5092	Let It Ride
5093	Let It Shine
5094	Let Me Bend Your Ear
5095	Let Me Break It Down Real Simple
5096	Let Me Count The Ways
5097	Let My People Go
5098	Let Nature Take Its Course
5099	Let Sleeping Dogs Lie
5100	Let The Buyer Beware
5101	Let The Cat Out Of The Bag
5102	Let The Chips Fall Where They May
5103	Let The Games Begin
5104	Let Them Eat Cake
5105	Let There Be Light
5106	Let Us Drink A Toast
5107	Let Your Hair Down
5108	Let's Be Careful Out There
5109	Let's Be Honest Here
5110	Let's Blow This Joint
5111	Let's Call It A Day
5112	Let's Change The World
5113	Let's Clear The Air
5114	Let's Cross That Bridge When We Come To It
5115	Let's Face It
5116	Let's Forge Ahead Shall We
5117	Let's Get America Moving Again
5118	Let's Get Down To Brass Tacks
5119	Let's Get It Off The Ground
5120	Let's Get Ready To Rumble
5121	Let's Get The Ball Rolling

95

5122	Let's Get This Plane Back To Washington
5123	Let's Get This Show On The Road
5124	Let's Get To The Bottom Of It
5125	Let's Go Dutch Treat
5126	Let's Have Sex
5127	Let's Head Out
5128	Let's Kill All The Lawyers
5129	Let's Move Forward
5130	Let's Play Zipper Tag
5131	Let's Rock & Roll All Night
5132	Let's Rock This Town
5133	Let's Roll
5134	Let's Run It Up The Flagpole And See Who Salutes It
5135	Let's Split
5136	Let's Take It From The Top
5137	Let's Talk Turkey
5138	Let's Tie The Knot
5139	Level Playing Field
5140	Liar Liar Pants Are On Fire
5141	Lick And A Promise
5142	Lick Into Shape
5143	Lickety Split
5144	Licking One's Wounds
5145	Lie Down With Dogs And Wake Up With Fleas
5146	Lie Down With Lions
5147	Lie Like A Rug
5148	Lie Through One's Teeth
5149	Life Begins At 40
5150	Life Goes On
5151	Life Imitates Art
5152	Life In The Fast Lane
5153	Life Is A Highway
5154	Life Is But A Dream
5155	Life Is Hard By The Yard But By The Inch It's A

	Cinch
5156	Life Is Just A Bowel Of Cherries
5157	Life Is Like A Box Of Chocolates You Never Know What You Are Going
5158	Life Is No Bed Of Roses
5159	Life Is Not About Working For Others
5160	Life Is Short And Sweet
5161	Life Is Short But It's Wide
5162	Life Is What You Make It
5163	Life Isn't All Beer And Skittles
5164	Life Liberty And The Pursuit Of Happiness
5165	Life Should Have A Purpose However Meaningless
5166	Life Stinks
5167	Life's What You Make It
5168	Life's A Banquet
5169	Life's A Beach
5170	Life's A Bitch
5171	Life's A Bowl Of Cherries
5172	Life's Little Miracles
5173	Life's Too Short
5174	Lift Yourself Up By Your Own Bootstraps
5175	Light A Fire Under It
5176	Light As A Feather
5177	Light At The End Of The Tunnel
5178	Light In The Loafers
5179	Light My Fire
5180	Lighter Than Air
5181	Lightning Never Strikes Twice In The Same Place
5182	Lights Are On But There's Nobody Home
5183	Lights Out

96

5184	Like A Bat Out Of Hell
5185	Like A Broken Record
5186	Like A Bull In A China Shop
5187	Like A Bump On A Log
5188	Like A Chicken With His Head Cut Off
5189	Like A Coiled Spring
5190	Like A Deer In Headlights
5191	Like A Dog Chasing Cars
5192	Like A Duck On A June Bug
5193	Like A Fish Out Of Water
5194	Like A Frog In A Frying Pan
5195	Like A Kid In A Candy Store
5196	Like A Knife Through Hot Butter
5197	Like A Lost Dog In The High Weeds
5198	Like A Trojan Horse
5199	Like A Virgin On Prom Night
5200	Like A Walk On The Beach
5201	Like Attracts Like
5202	Like Balling The Jack
5203	Like Butter
5204	Like Chalk And Cheese
5205	Like Clockwork
5206	Like Drawing Bees To Honey
5207	Like Father Like Son
5208	Like Flies On Shit
5209	Like Getting Your Tit In The Wringer
5210	Like It Or Not
5211	Like It's Going Out Of Style
5212	Like Lambs To The Slaughterhouse
5213	Like Looking For A Needle In A Haystack
5214	Like Mother Like Daughter
5215	Like Night And Day
5216	Like Oil And Water

5217	Like Peas In A Pod
5218	Like Pigs In A Poke
5219	Like Pulling Teeth
5220	Like Putty In Your Hands
5221	Like Shit Off A Shovel
5222	Like Shooting Ducks On A Pond
5223	Like Shooting Fish In A Barrel
5224	Like Taking Candy From A Baby
5225	Like The Back Of My Hand
5226	Like There Is No Tomorrow
5227	Like Two Peas In A Pod
5228	Like Walking On Eggshells
5229	Like Water Off A Duck's Back
5230	Like White On Rice
5231	Limited Only By Your Imagination
5232	Line In The Sand
5233	Line Your Pockets
5234	Lion's Den
5235	Lion's Share
5236	Lipstick On A Pig
5237	Listen To Me Very Carefully
5238	Listen Up
5239	Lit To The Gills
5240	Litmus Test
5241	Little Bird Told Me
5242	Little Black Book
5243	Little Of This Little Of That
5244	Little Strokes Fell Great Oaks
5245	Live And Learn
5246	Live And Let Live
5247	Live Everyday As Though It Were Your Last
5248	Live Life To The Max
5249	Live Long And Prosper
5250	Live To Fight Another Day
5251	Live Without Fear

97

5252	Live Your Life
5253	Livin' On A Prayer
5254	Livin' On The Edge
5255	Living A Charmed Life
5256	Living Hand To Mouth
5257	Living High Off The Hog
5258	Living In A Cloud
5259	Living In An Ivory Tower
5260	Living The Good Life
5261	Living The Life Of Riley
5262	Living The Life You've Always Dreamed Of
5263	Living The Secret Life
5264	Lo And Behold
5265	Loaded For Bear
5266	Lock And Load
5267	Lock 'Em Up And Through Away The Key
5268	Lock Stock And Barrel
5269	Long And Short Of It
5270	Long Arm Of The Law
5271	Long Hard Row To Hoe
5272	Long In The Tooth
5273	Long Live The King
5274	Long Row To Hoe
5275	Long Shot
5276	Long Time No See
5277	Long Way Around
5278	Long Ways Away
5279	Look Before You Leap
5280	Look Down Your Nose At Someone
5281	Look Into Your Heart
5282	Look Like Death Warmed Over
5283	Look Out
5284	Look Out For Number One
5285	Look Over Your Shoulder
5286	Look Up In The Sky It's
5287	Lookin' For A Good Time

5288	Looking At The World Through Rosy Colored Glasses
5289	Looking Down The Barrel Of A Gun
5290	Looking For A Needle In A Haystack
5291	Looking In All The Wrong Places
5292	Looking Through Your Eyes
5293	Looks Can Be Deceiving
5294	Looks Like There's A New Sheriff In Town
5295	Loop Hole
5296	Looped
5297	Loose Cannon
5298	Loose Lips Sink Ships
5299	Loose Your Shirt
5300	Looser
5301	Lord Gives And Takes Away
5302	Lord Willin' And The Creek Don't Rise
5303	Lordy Be
5304	Lose Face
5305	Lose The Tights
5306	Lose Your Lunch
5307	Lose Your Shirt
5308	Lost A Step
5309	Lost In Love
5310	Lots Of Honey Makes Bees Lazy
5311	Loud And Clear
5312	Loud As All Get Out
5313	Love And Hate Are Two Horns On The Same Goat
5314	Love Conquers All
5315	Love Don't Live Here
5316	Love Handles

98

5317	Love Is A Many Splendored Thing
5318	Love Is A Temporary Insanity Curable By Marriage
5319	Love Is Blind
5320	Love Is Magical
5321	Love Makes The World Go Round
5322	Love Me Love My Dog
5323	Love Means Never Having To Say You're Sorry
5324	Love Of Money Is The Root Of All Evil
5325	Love Thy Neighbor
5326	Love Will Keep Us Together
5327	Love Will Save The Day
5328	Love Your Neighbor As You Love Yourself
5329	Low Man On The Totem Pole
5330	Lower Than A Snake's Belly
5331	Lower The Boom
5332	Luck Is The Residue Of Design
5333	Luck Of The Draw
5334	Lucky Stiff
5335	Lucky To Be Alive
5336	Lying Through Your Teeth
5337	Mad As A Hatter
5338	Mad As A Wet Hen
5339	Mad Cap
5340	Madder Than A Wet Hen
5341	Made In The Shade
5342	Made It By The Skin Of My Teeth
5343	Made It Ma To The Top Of The World
5344	Made Of Money
5345	Mail It In
5346	Main Dish
5347	Main Drag
5348	Main Liner
5349	Make A Big Deal Out Of Nothing
5350	Make A Break For It
5351	Make A Fast Buck
5352	Make A Long Story Short
5353	Make A Mountain Out Of A Molehill
5354	Make A Statement Without Saying A Word
5355	Make A Virtue Of Necessity
5356	Make An Ass Out Of Yourself
5357	Make Em Laugh
5358	Make Ends Meet
5359	Make Eye Contact
5360	Make Haste Slowly
5361	Make Hay While The Sun Shines
5362	Make Heads Or Tails Of It
5363	Make It Happen
5364	Make It Or Break It
5365	Make Like A Baby And Head Out
5366	Make Like A Tree And Leave
5367	Make Like A Tree And Leave It Up To Someone Else
5368	Make Me
5369	Make Money Hand Over Fist
5370	Make My Day
5371	Make No Bones About It
5372	Make One's Mouth Water
5373	Make Or Break
5374	Make Out Like A Bandit
5375	Make The Grade
5376	Make The Most Out Of It
5377	Make The Season Bright
5378	Make The World Go Away

99

5379	Make Tracks
5380	Make Up
5381	Make Waves
5382	Make Your Hair Stand On End
5383	Make Your Mark
5384	Make Your Move
5385	Makes A Man Healthy Wealthy And Wise
5386	Makes My Blood Boil
5387	Makes My Heart Skip A Beat
5388	Makin' Bacon
5389	Makin' Whoopie
5390	Making A Mountain Out Of A Molehill
5391	Making A Quick Buck
5392	Making Ends Meet
5393	Making Hay
5394	Making Him Sing Like A Canary
5395	Making Money Across The Board
5396	Making Money Hand Over Fist
5397	Making The Beast With Two Backs
5398	Man Does Not Live By Bread Alone
5399	Man For All Seasons
5400	Man I Feel Like A Woman
5401	Man Is As Old As He Feels
5402	Man On The Moon
5403	Man Plans And God Laughs
5404	Manic Monday
5405	Manner Born
5406	Manners Make The Man
5407	Man's Best Friend
5408	Man's Home Is His Castle
5409	Many Are Called But Few Are Chosen
5410	Many Clubs Have A Question Mark In The Shape Of An Axe
5411	Many Hands Make Light Work
5412	Many Happy Returns
5413	Many Little Things Add Up To Something Big
5414	March Comes In Like A Lion And Goes Out Like A Lamb
5415	March To The Beat Of A Different Drummer
5416	Marching To A Different Drummer
5417	Marcia Marcia Marcia
5418	Mares Eat Oats And Does Eat Oats
5419	Margaritaville
5420	Mark My Words
5421	Mark This Place And Time
5422	Marked Man
5423	Marking Time
5424	Marriage Is A Sort Of Friendship
5425	Marriage Of Two Minds
5426	Marriages Are Made In Heaven
5427	Marry In Haste Repent In Leisure
5428	Matter Of Fact
5429	May The Force Be With You
5430	Maybe Something Will Jog Your Memory
5431	Mean As A Snake
5432	Measure Twice Cut Once
5433	Meet And Greet
5434	Meet Me Halfway
5435	Meet Your Waterloo
5436	Melting Pot
5437	Memory Like An Elephant

100

5438	Mercy Me	5470	Money Doesn't Grow On Trees
5439	Me Thinks She Doth Protest Too Much	5471	Money Grubbing
5440	Mexican Standoff	5472	Money Has No Smell
5441	Mi Casa Es Su Casa	5473	Money Hungry
5442	Might As Well Can't Dance	5474	Money Hungry Be
5443	Might As Well Throw In The Towel	5475	Money In The Bank
		5476	Money Is No Object
5444	Might Makes Right	5477	Money Is Power
5445	Mile High Club	5478	Money Is The Root Of All Evil
5446	Milk It For All It's Worth	5479	Money Isn't Everything But It Sure Helps
5447	Milk The Bird In Your Hand		
5448	Milking It For All It's Worth	5480	Money Isn't What It Used To Be
5449	Million To One		
5450	Milquetoast	5481	Money Isn't Worth The Paper It's Printed On
5451	Mind Over Matter		
5452	Mind Your Manners	5482	Money Loves Company
5453	Mind Your Own Beeswax	5483	Money Makes Money
5454	Mind Your Own Business	5484	Money Makes The World Go Round
5455	Mind Your P's And Q's		
5456	Mini Me	5485	Money Talks
5457	Misery Loves Company	5486	Money Talks An Bullshit Walks
5458	Misery Makes Strange Bedfellows	5487	Money Talks But All Mine Ever Says Is Goodbye
5459	Miss The Boat	5488	Money Up The Wazoo
5460	Missed By A Hair	5489	Monkey Business
5461	Missed The Boat	5490	Monkey See Monkey Do
5462	Mission Critical	5491	Monkey With
5463	Mixed Feeling About It	5492	Monkey Wrench
5464	Mom Always Liked You Best	5493	Monkeying Around
		5494	Month In And Month Out
5465	Money Begets Money	5495	Mony A Mickle Maks A Muckle
5466	Money Burns A Hole In His Pocket		
		5496	Moon Shine
5467	Money Can't Buy Happiness	5497	Moon Struck
		5498	More Bang For The Buck
5468	Money Can't Buy You Happiness	5499	More Cliches Than You Can Shake A Stick At
5469	Money Can't Buy You Love		

5500	More Fun Than A Barrel Of Monkeys	5533	My Hair Was On End
5501	More Power To You	5534	My Hair Was On The Edge Of Its Seat
5502	More Than Meets The Eye	5535	My Hands Are Tied
5503	More Than Skin Deep	5536	My Hat's Off To You
5504	More The Merrier	5537	My Head Is Swimming
5505	More Things Change More They Stay The Same	5538	My Heart Sank
5506	More Valuable Than Gold	5539	My Lips Are Sealed
5507	More We Learn Less We Know	5540	My Little Black Book
		5541	My Mama Always Said
5508	Most Popular Kid In School	5542	My Precious
5509	Mother Of Mercy	5543	My Stomach Is Tied Up In Knots
5510	Mouth Off	5544	My Way Or The Highway
5511	Move That Bus	5545	My Wish Came True
5512	Move The Needle	5546	Nail Biter
5513	Moves To The Beat Of A Different Drummer	5547	Nail Your Colors To The Mast
5514	Moving At A Snail's Pace	5548	Naked As A Jaybird
5515	Mr. Gorbachev Tear Down This Wall	5549	Naked As The Day You Were Born
5516	Much Ado About Nothing	5550	Naked Truth
5517	Much Better Than Apple Pie	5551	Namby Pamby
		5552	Name Of The Game
5518	Much To Do About Nothing	5553	Name That Tune
5519	Mud Slinging	5554	Name Your Poison
5520	Mug For The Camera	5555	Nary A Word Was Spoken
5521	Mum's The Word	5556	Nature Abhors A Vacuum
5522	Murder Will Out	5557	Nature Of The Beast
5523	Murphy's Law	5558	Nature's First Green Is Gold
5524	Music Hath The Power To Soothe The Savage Beast	5559	Near And Dear To My Heart
5525	Must Be Seeing Things	5560	Necessary Evil
5526	My Bad	5561	Necessity Is The Mother Of Invention
5527	My Brain Is Fried	5562	Necessity Knows No Laws
5528	My Bread And Butter	5563	Need Some Milk Money
5529	My Country Right Or Wrong	5564	Needle In A Haystack
5530	My Cup Runneth Over	5565	Neither A Borrower Not A Lender Be
5531	My Dear I Don't Give A Damn	5566	Neither Fish Nor Fowl
5532	My Dogs Are Barking		

5567	Neither Give Nor Take Offense
5568	Neither Head Nor Tail
5569	Neither Here Nor There
5570	Neither Hide Nor Hair
5571	Neither Rhyme Nor Reason
5572	Nero Fiddled While Rome Burned
5573	Nerves Of Steel
5574	Nervous As A Cat On A Hot Tin Roof
5575	Nervous As A Long Tailed Cat In A Room Full Of Rocking Chairs
5576	Never Assume
5577	Never Believe Everything You Hear
5578	Never Cry Wolf
5579	Never Give A Sucker An Even Break
5580	Never Had It So Good
5581	Never Have To Work Another Day In Your Life
5582	Never Hurts To Try
5583	Never In A Month Of Sundays
5584	Never Judge A Book By It's Cove (Including This One)
5585	Never Let Your Left Hand Know What Your Right Hand's Doing
5586	Never Look A Gift Horse In The Mouth
5587	Never Mix Business With Pleasure
5588	Never Pet A Burning Dog
5589	Never Put Off Until Tomorrow What You Can Do Today
5590	Never Say Die
5591	Never Say Never

5592	Never Sell America Short
5593	Never Speak Ill Of The Dead
5594	Never Take A Shower With A Cat Duct Taped To Your Chest
5595	Never Tell Tales Out Of School
5596	Never Too Late To Learn
5597	New Jobs Available
5598	New Kid On The Block
5599	New Lease On Life
5600	New Media Is The New Math
5601	Newbie
5602	Next To Nothing
5603	Nice Cage No Bird
5604	Nice Day For A Picnic
5605	Nice Guys Finish Last
5606	Nice Play Shakespeare
5607	Nice Work If You Can Get It
5608	Nickel And Dime
5609	Night And Day Like
5610	Nin Com Poop
5611	Nip And Tuck
5612	Nip It In The Bud
5613	Nitty Gritty
5614	No Accounting For Taste
5615	No Alibis
5616	No Bad Deed Goes Unpunished
5617	No Brainer
5618	No Chalk From Cheese
5619	No Dice
5620	No Doubt About It
5621	No Go
5622	No Good To Fight But If Must Fight Win
5623	No Great Shakes
5624	No Guts No Glory
5625	No Holds Barred
5626	No Ifs Ands Or Buts

5627	No If's And's Or Butt's About It		5662	Not A Ring Of Truth
5628	No Interest No Payment		5663	Not A Snowball's Chance In Hell
5629	No Investment No Gain		5664	Not A Spinning Wheels In The Kingdom Prick Your Fingers
5630	No Man Can Serve Two Masters			
5631	No Man Is A Hero To His Valet		5665	Not All Cracked Up To Be
5632	No Man Is An Island		5666	Not Always Black And White
5633	No News Is Good News		5667	Not By The Hair On My Chinny Chin Chin
5634	No One Here But Us Chickens			
5635	No One Is Above The Law		5668	Not Enough Room To Swing A Cat
5636	No One Is Perfect		5669	Not Even
5637	No One Needs To Know		5670	Not For All The Tea In China
5638	No One's Fault But My Own			
5639	No Out Of Pocket Costs		5671	Not For Nothing
5640	No Pain No Gain		5672	Not In A Million Years
5641	No Person Is Indispensable		5673	Not Just Another Pretty Face
5642	No Problem			
5643	No Rest For The Wicked		5674	Not Just Whistling Dixie
5644	No Shit Sherlock		5675	Not Much Grass Grows On A Busy Street
5645	No Skin Off My Back			
5646	No Skin Off My Nose		5676	Not My Cup Of Tea
5647	No Soup For You		5677	Not One Iota
5648	No Strings Attached		5678	Not Playing With A Full Deck
5649	No Sweat			
5650	No Time To Waste		5679	Not Rowing With Both Oars
5651	No Use Crying Over Spilled Milk		5680	Not The Brightest Bulb In The Chandelier
5652	No Victory Without A Battle		5681	Not The Brightest Crayon In The Box
5653	No Way José			
5654	No Way On God's Green Earth		5682	Not The Ghost Of A Chance
5655	No Where To Hide		5683	Not The Sharpest Crayon In The Box
5656	Nobody Is Infallible			
5657	Nobody Puts Baby In The Corner		5684	Not The Sharpest Knife In The Cabinet
5658	Nod Off		5685	Not The Sharpest Pencil In The Box
5659	None Of Your Business			
5660	None Too Pleased		5686	Not To Know Someone From Adam
5661	Noodle On		5687	Not To Turn A Hair

104

5688	Not Tonight Honey
5689	Not Whether You Win Or Lose But How You Play The Game
5690	Not Worth A Hill Of Beans
5691	Not Worth A Rap
5692	Not Worth A Tinker's Dam
5693	Nothin' But A Good Time
5694	Nothing Comes From Nothing
5695	Nothing Could Be Further From The Truth
5696	Nothing Happens Purely By Accident
5697	Nothing Happens Until Something Sells
5698	Nothing Held Back
5699	Nothing Human Is Alien To Me
5700	Nothing Hurts Like The Truth
5701	Nothing Is Certain But Death And Taxes
5702	Nothing Is Impossible For Those Who Don't Have To Do It Themselves
5703	Nothing Isn't Free
5704	Nothing New Under The Sun
5705	Nothing Personal
5706	Nothing Succeeds Like Success
5707	Nothing To Fear But Fear Itself
5708	Nothing To Sneeze At
5709	Nothing To Write Home About
5710	Nothing Up My Sleeve
5711	Nothing Ventured Nothing Gained
5712	Now Cut That Out
5713	Now Is The Time For All Good Men To Come To The Aid Of Their County
5714	Now It's Gone Too Far
5715	Now More Than Ever
5716	Now Or Never
5717	Now Or Never It's
5718	Now This Won't Hurt A Bit
5719	Now You Put Your Foot In It
5720	Now You See It Now You Don't
5721	Now You're In The Catbird Seat
5722	Now's As Good A Time As Any
5723	Now's The Best Time
5724	Now's Your Chance
5725	Num Skull
5726	Numb As A Hake
5727	Number Crunching
5728	Number One
5729	Nutty As A Fruitcake
5730	Object Of Desire
5731	Odd Sock Seeks Match
5732	Of Biblical Proportions
5733	Off And Running
5734	Off Base
5735	Off Kilter
5736	Off Like A Prom Dress
5737	Off The Cuff
5738	Off The Dime
5739	Off The Face Of The Earth
5740	Off The Hook
5741	Off The Shelf
5742	Off The Top Of My Head
5743	Off The Wagon
5744	Off With His Head
5745	Off Your Hinges
5746	Off Your Perch
5747	Off Your Rocker
5748	Offense Is

105

	The Best Defense
5749	Often A Bridesmaid Never A Bride
5750	Oh Brother
5751	Oh My
5752	Oh My Ears And Whiskers
5753	Oh My God
5754	Oh My God They Killed It
5755	Oh My Goodness
5756	Oh My Nose
5757	Oh No Mr. Bill
5758	Oh No Not Again
5759	Oh Romeo Romeo Wherefore Art Thou Romeo
5760	Oh To Be A Fly On The Wall
5761	Oh Woe Is Me
5762	Oil And Water Don't Mix
5763	OK That Does it
5764	Okey Dokey
5765	Old As Dirt
5766	Old As The Hills
5767	Old Ball And Chain
5768	Old Blowhard
5769	Old Fogey
5770	Old Habits Die Hard
5771	Old School
5772	Old Soldiers Never Die They Just Fade Away
5773	Old Standby
5774	Old Stomping Grounds
5775	Old Time Rock And Roll
5776	Old Wives Tale
5777	Old-Boy Network
5778	On A Lark
5779	On A Roll
5780	On A Shoestring
5781	On A Shoestring Budget
5782	On A Short Leash
5783	On A Silver Platter
5784	On A Slow Boat To China
5785	On A Soap Box

5786	On A Wild Goose Chase
5787	On A Wing And A Prayer
5788	On Bended Knee
5789	On Cloud Nine
5790	On Easy Street
5791	On Equal Footing
5792	On Fire
5793	On Him Like Ugly On An Ape
5794	On Par
5795	On Pins And Needles
5796	On Skid Row
5797	On Tenterhooks
5798	On The Back Burner
5799	On The Ball
5800	On The Cutting Edge
5801	On The Double
5802	On The Edge Of Your Seat
5803	On The Flip Side
5804	On The Fly
5805	On The Fritz
5806	On The Front Burner
5807	On The Horizon
5808	On The House
5809	On The Level
5810	On The Make
5811	On The Nail
5812	On The Nose
5813	On The One Hand
5814	On The Other Hand
5815	On The Road
5816	On The Road Again
5817	On The Rocks
5818	On The Run
5819	On The Same Page
5820	On The Same Plate
5821	On The Straight And Narrow
5822	On The Take
5823	On The Tip Of My Tongue
5824	On The Up And Up

5825	On The Wagon
5826	On To Something
5827	On Track Be
5828	On Ya Bike
5829	On Your Toes
5830	Once A Thief Always A Thief
5831	Once Bitten Twice Shy
5832	Once Burned Twice Shy
5833	Once In A Blue Moon
5834	Once In A Coon's Age
5835	Once In A Dog's Age
5836	Once In A Lifetime
5837	Once More Onto The Beaches Dear Friends
5838	Once Upon A Time
5839	One Bad Apple Spoils The Whole Barrel
5840	One Brick Short Of A Load
5841	One Day At A Time
5842	One Foot In The Grave
5843	One Foot On A Banana Peel The Other In The Grave
5844	One For The Books
5845	One For The Road
5846	One Good Turn Deserves Another
5847	One Hand Washes The Other
5848	One Horse Open Sleigh
5849	One Horse Town
5850	One In Million
5851	One Lie Leads To Another
5852	One Man's Foul Weather Is Another Man's Fair
5853	One Man's Garbage Is Another Man's Treasure
5854	One Man's Lose Is Another Man's Gain
5855	One Man's Meat Is Another Man's Poison

5856	One Man's Trash Is Another Man's Treasure
5857	One More Such Victory And We Are Lost
5858	One More Thing
5859	One Must Crawl Before He Walks
5860	One Nation Under God
5861	One Night Stand
5862	One Of A Kind
5863	One Picture Is Worth A Thousand Words
5864	One Rotten Apple Spoils The Barrel
5865	One Size Fits All
5866	One Small Step For Man One Giant Leap For Mankind
5867	One Step At A Time
5868	One Swallow Does Not Make A Summer
5869	One Sweet Day
5870	One Taco Short Of A Combination Plate
5871	One Toe Over The Line
5872	One Tough Cookie
5873	One Track Mind
5874	One Two Punch
5875	One Way Or Another
5876	One Way Out
5877	Only A Couple Hours A Week
5878	Only God Knows Why
5879	Only The Good Die Young
5880	Only Unsolvable Problems Are Worthy Of Artificial Intelligence
5881	Only Women Bleed
5882	Oops! I Did It Again
5883	Oopsy Daisy
5884	Open A Can Of Worms
5885	Open A Keg Of Nails

5886	Open And Shut Case
5887	Open Mouth Closed Mind
5888	Open Pandora's Box
5889	Open The Kimono
5890	Open The Pod Bay Doors Hal
5891	Open Up A Can Of Whoop Ass
5892	Open Your Eyes
5893	Opened A Can Of Worms
5894	Opening The Floodgates
5895	Opportunity Doesn't Knock Twice
5896	Opportunity Knocks But Once
5897	Opposites Attract
5898	Other Fish To Fry
5899	Our Go To Guys
5900	Our Minds Are Like Parachutes
5901	Our Product Is Best Because All The Others Are Wrong
5902	Out For A Sunday Stroll
5903	Out Like A Light
5904	Out Of Gas
5905	Out Of It
5906	Out Of It Be
5907	Out Of Pocket
5908	Out Of Sight Out Of Mind
5909	Out Of The Blue
5910	Out Of The Clear Blue
5911	Out Of The Frying Pan And Into The Fire
5912	Out Of The Mouths Of Babes Comes Great Truth
5913	Out Of The Pot And Into The Kettle
5914	Out Of The Prying Pan Into The Fire
5915	Out Of The Woods
5916	Out Of Whack

5917	Out On A Limb
5918	Out Sowing Your Wild Oats
5919	Out To Lunch
5920	Out With The Bath Water
5921	Out With The Old In With The New
5922	Over A Barrel
5923	Over And Done With
5924	Over And Out
5925	Over And Over Again
5926	Over Hill And Dale
5927	Over My Dead Body
5928	Over My Head
5929	Over Stepping Your Boundaries
5930	Over The Edge
5931	Over The Hill
5932	Over The Top
5933	Pack It In
5934	Packing Heat
5935	Packing Lead
5936	Paddle One's Own Canoe
5937	Paddy Whack
5938	Pain At The Pump
5939	Pain In The Ass
5940	Pain In The Butt
5941	Pain In The Neck
5942	Paint Oneself Into A Corner
5943	Paint The Town Red
5944	Paint Your Dream
5945	Paint Yourself Into A Corner
5946	Pan Out
5947	Pandemonium Broke Loose
5948	Pandora's Box
5949	Paper Bleeds Little
5950	Paper Over
5951	Paper Tiger
5952	Par For The Course
5953	Pardon Me Would You Have Any Grey Poupon

5954	Part And Parcel	5990	Peeping Tom
5955	Parting Is Such Sweet Sorrow	5991	Pen Is Mightier Than The Sword
5956	Party Pooper	5992	Pencil It In
5957	Pass Away	5993	Pencil Me In
5958	Pass On	5994	Pennies From Heaven
5959	Pass The Acid Test	5995	Pennies On The Dollar
5960	Pass The Buck	5996	Penny For Your Thoughts
5961	Pass The Gravy	5997	Penny Pincher
5962	Pass The Hat	5998	Penny Saved Is A Penny Earned
5963	Pass The Hooch		
5964	Pass The Plate	5999	Penny Wise And Pound Foolish
5965	Passed The Test Of Time		
5966	Passed With Flying Colors	6000	People Come People Go
5967	Passing The Buck	6001	People Want Stupid
5968	Past Present And Future	6002	People Who Live In Glass Houses Shouldn't Throw Stones
5969	Pat On The Back		
5970	Path Of Least Resistance	6003	Perception Becomes Reality
5971	Patience Is A Virtue		
5972	Pay A King's Ransom	6004	Perfect Practice Makes Perfect
5973	Pay An Arm And A Leg		
5974	Pay As You Go	6005	Persnickety
5975	Pay Attention To Details	6006	Person's Life Is Like A TV Show
5976	Pay Lip Service		
5977	Pay The Dept Of Nature	6007	Peter Out
5978	Pay The Piper	6008	Petered Out
5979	Pay The Piper His Due	6009	Phone It In
5980	Pay Through The Nose	6010	Physician Heal Thy Self
5981	Pay Your Money And Take Your Choice	6011	Pick Of The Litter
		6012	Pick Over The Ruins
5982	Payback Is A Bitch	6013	Pick The Low Hanging Fruit
5983	Peace On Earth Good Will Toward Men	6014	Pick Yourself Up And Dust Yourself Off
		6015	Picking Up The Pace
5984	Peaches And Cream Complexion	6016	Picking Up The Tab
		6017	Picture Perfect
5985	Pearls Before Swine	6018	Picture's Worth A Thousand Words
5986	Pee Or Get Off The Pot		
5987	Peek Under The Hood	6019	Pie In The Sky
5988	Peel Back The Onion	6020	Piece Of Cake
5989	Peel Out		

109

6021	Pieces Of Eight
6022	Pig And Whistle
6023	Pig Dog
6024	Pig Headed
6025	Pig In A Poke
6026	Pig In A Python
6027	Pig Out
6028	Piggy Back
6029	Piggy Bank
6030	Pigs Are Pigs
6031	Pin Money
6032	Pin Our Hopes On
6033	Pin Your Hopes On Something
6034	Pinch A Loaf
6035	Pipe Down
6036	Pipe Dream
6037	Piss Poor
6038	Pissed To The Gills
6039	Pissing In The Wind
6040	Pistol Packin Mama
6041	Place For Everything And Everything In Its Place
6042	Plain And Simple
6043	Plain As A Rainy Tuesday
6044	Plain As Day
6045	Plane As The Nose On Your Face
6046	Plant A Seed Of Friendship Reap A Bouquet Of Happiness
6047	Plastered
6048	Play Both Ends Against The Middle
6049	Play Cat And Mouse
6050	Play Fast And Loose
6051	Play For The Name On The Front Of Your Jersey
6052	Play Hardball
6053	Play Hooky
6054	Play Hot Potato

6055	Play It Again Sam (Play it Once Sam For Old Times' sake)
6056	Play It By Ear
6057	Play It Smart
6058	Play Second Fiddle
6059	Play The Cards You're Dealt
6060	Play The Field
6061	Play The Final Card
6062	Play The Hand You're Dealt
6063	Play The Race Card
6064	Play With The Big Boys
6065	Played Me For A Fool
6066	Playing By The Rules
6067	Playing Possum
6068	Playing Second Filddle
6069	Playing The Field
6070	Playing To The Gallery
6071	Playing With Fire
6072	Playing With Loaded Dice
6073	Pleased As Punch
6074	Plenty Of Fish In The Ocean
6075	Plenty Of Other Fish In The Sea Have
6076	Plenty Of Other Fish To Fry
6077	Plenty To Go 'Round
6078	Pluck Your Magic Twanger Froggy
6079	Plucked From Thin Air
6080	Plunk Down
6081	Poets Are Born Not Made
6082	Point Blank
6083	Poison The Well
6084	Poker Face
6085	Pole Cat
6086	Politics Make Strange Bedfellows
6087	Polluted
6088	Polly Anna

6089	Polly Want A Cracker
6090	Poor As A Church Mouse
6091	Pop A Top
6092	Pop A Vein
6093	Pop Goes The Weasel
6094	Pork Barrel
6095	Porter House
6096	Possession Is Nine Tenths Of The Law
6097	Pot Calling The Kettle Black
6098	Pot Of Gold At The End Of The Rainbow
6099	Pound For Pound
6100	Pound Of Flesh
6101	Pound The Pavement
6102	Pound The Table
6103	Pour It On Thick
6104	Pour Oil On Trouble Waters
6105	Pour Some Sugar On Me
6106	Pour The Kool Aid
6107	Poverty Is No Sin
6108	Power Corrupts
6109	Power Lunch
6110	Power To The People
6111	Powers Of Darkness
6112	Practice Makes Perfect
6113	Practice What You Preach
6114	Praise The Bridge That Carries You Over
6115	Praise The Lord And Pass The Ammunition
6116	Pray To The Porcelain God
6117	Preach The Choir
6118	Preach To The Converted
6119	Preaching To The Choir
6120	Press The Flesh
6121	Pretty As A Picture
6122	Pretty Is As Pretty Does
6123	Pretty Kettle Of Fish
6124	Pretty Penny

6125	Pretty Pickle
6126	Prevention Is Better Than The Cure
6127	Prevention Is Better Than Treatment
6128	Priced To Sell
6129	Pride Goes Before A Fall
6130	Primed To The Sticking Point
6131	Procrastination Is The Thief Of Time
6132	Proof Is In The Pudding
6133	Propped Up
6134	Prosperity Is Just Around The Corner
6135	Proud As Sin
6136	Proud Flesh
6137	Providing A Helping Hand
6138	Psych
6139	Pull A Boner
6140	Pull A Fast One
6141	Pull A Rabbit Out Of A Hat
6142	Pull Any Stunts
6143	Pull Back The Curtain
6144	Pull In One's Horns
6145	Pull Out All The Stops
6146	Pull Strings
6147	Pull The Wool Over Your Eyes
6148	Pull Up By The Bootstraps
6149	Pull Up Stakes
6150	Pull Your Finger Out
6151	Pull Your Head Out Of Your Ass
6152	Pull Your Leg
6153	Pull Yourself Up By Your Own Bootstraps
6154	Pulled Out Of Thin Air
6155	Pulling Your Hair
6156	Pulling Your Leg
6157	Pump Up The Volume

6158	Punch His Lights Out
6159	Punched In The Gut
6160	Punctuality Is The Politeness Of Kings
6161	Pure As The Driven Snow
6162	Push It To The Limit
6163	Push Your Buttons
6164	Pushing The Envelope
6165	Pushing Up Daisies
6166	Put A Cork In It
6167	Put A Lid On It
6168	Put A Little Elbow Grease Into It
6169	Put A Monkey Wrench In The Works
6170	Put A Sock In It
6171	Put First Things First
6172	Put In One's Best Licks
6173	Put It In The Hopper
6174	Put It Through Its Paces
6175	Put My Two Cents In
6176	Put On A Happy Face
6177	Put On Ice
6178	Put On Ice To Cool Off
6179	Put On The Back Burner
6180	Put On Your Thinking Cap
6181	Put Out Some Feelers
6182	Put Out The Fire
6183	Put That In Your Pipe And Smoke It
6184	Put The Bite On
6185	Put The Finger On You
6186	Put The Hammer Down
6187	Put The Pedal To The Metal
6188	Put The Screws On
6189	Put Two And Two Together
6190	Put Up Or Shut Up
6191	Put Up Your Feet And Stay Awhile
6192	Put Your Best Foot Forward

6193	Put Your Cards On The Table
6194	Put Your Foot In Your Mouth
6195	Put Your Head In The Sand
6196	Put Your Head On My Shoulder
6197	Put Your Heart Into It
6198	Put Your Money On The Line
6199	Put Your Money Where Your Mouth Is
6200	Put Your Nose To The Grindstone
6201	Put Your Shoulder To The Wheel
6202	Put Your Toe In The Water
6203	Puts Them On The Map
6204	Putting His Feet To The Fire
6205	Putting It All On The Line
6206	Putting On The Dog
6207	Putting The Cart Before The Horse
6208	Putting The Screws To Him
6209	Quacking In Their Boots
6210	Quagmire
6211	Quality Speaks Volumes
6212	Quarter Back
6213	Quarter Horse
6214	Queen For A Day
6215	Queer As A Three-Dollar Bill
6216	Quick Buck
6217	Quicker Than A New York Minute
6218	Quid Pro Quo
6219	Quiet As A Church Mouse
6220	Quiet As A Mouse
6221	Quiet As A Mouse Dropping A Pinful Of Angels
6222	Quiet On The Set

6223	Quit Horsing Around
6224	Quit Playing Games
6225	Quit While You're Ahead
6226	Quit Your Belly Aching
6227	Rag Tag
6228	Rag Time
6229	Rags To Riches
6230	Rain Or Shine
6231	Raining Cats And Dogs
6232	Raining Pitchforks
6233	Raise Cain
6234	Raise The Bar
6235	Raise The Dead
6236	Raise The Mizenmast Full Speed Ahead
6237	Raise The Roof
6238	Raise Your Hand
6239	Raising Cain
6240	Raising The Bar
6241	Raking In The Dough
6242	Raking In The Money
6243	Raking It In
6244	Rally Round
6245	Ram Shackled
6246	Rambunctious
6247	Ramp Up
6248	Rat Hole
6249	Rat Out
6250	Rats Desert A Sinking Ship
6251	Rattle The Rafters
6252	Rattle Trap
6253	Rattle Your Cage
6254	Raw End Of The Deal
6255	Reach The Right Market With The Right Message
6256	Read Between The Lines
6257	Read Him The Riot Act
6258	Read It And Weep
6259	Read My Lips No New Taxes
6260	Read The Fine Print

6261	Read The Handwriting On The Wall
6262	Read The Riot Act
6263	Read You Him The Riot Act
6264	Ready For Love
6265	Ready To Spill The Beans
6266	Real Gulley Washer
6267	Real McCoy
6268	Real Toad Strangler
6269	Real Wing Dinger
6270	Really Bugging Me
6271	Red Carpet Treatment
6272	Red Carpet Treatment The
6273	Red Herring
6274	Red Letter Day
6275	Red Neck
6276	Red Sky In The Morning Sailor's Warning - Red Sky At Night Sailor's Delight
6277	Remember Me
6278	Remember The Alamo
6279	Remember When
6280	Render Unto Caesar The Things Which Are Caesar's
6281	Reopen An Old Wound
6282	Report Of My Death Are Greatly Exaggerated
6283	Resistance Is Futile
6284	Resistance To Change
6285	Rest Assured
6286	Rest On Your Laurels
6287	Resting On One's Laurels
6288	Return To Sender
6289	Revenge Is Sweet
6290	Revolutionary Approach
6291	Rhyme Or Reason
6292	Rich And Poor Alike
6293	Ride Of Into The Sunset
6294	Ride Roughshod Over
6295	Ride The Gravy Train
6296	Riding For A Fall

113

6297	Riding On	6333	Roll Out The Red Carpet
6298	Riding The Wild Pony	6334	Roll Over Beethoven
6299	Riff Raff	6335	Roll Over In His Grave
6300	Rifle For An Arm	6336	Roll With The Punches
6301	Right As A Trivet	6337	Rolling In Money
6302	Right As Rain	6338	Rolling In The Dough
6303	Right Before Your Eyes	6339	Rolling Stone Gathers No Moss
6304	Right Down Your Alley		
6305	Right Frame Of Mind	6340	Rollover On
6306	Right In Front Of You	6341	Rome Wasn't Built In A Day
6307	Right Off The Bat	6342	Rope Of Sand
6308	Right Off The Top Of Your Head	6343	Rosebud
		6344	Rotten To The Core
6309	Right On The Button	6345	Rough Around The Edges
6310	Right On The Dot	6346	Rough As A Cob
6311	Right On The Money	6347	Rough Road
6312	Right On The Nose	6348	Round Robin
6313	Right Or Wrong It's A Message	6349	Round The Bend
		6350	Round Up The Usual Suspects
6314	Right Out From Under Them		
		6351	Rub It In
6315	Right To Your Front Doorstep	6352	Rub Salt In The Wound
		6353	Rub Your Nose In It
6316	Right Under Your Nose	6354	Rubber Neck
6317	Right Up Your Alley	6355	Rubbing Elbows
6318	Ring A Bell	6356	Rubbing Salt In His Wounds
6319	Ring In The New Year		
6320	Ring Your Bell	6357	Rubs Me The Wrong Way
6321	Rise And Shine	6358	Rule Of Thumb
6322	Rising Tide	6359	Rule The Roost
6323	Rising Tide Lifts All Boats	6360	Rule With An Iron Fist
6324	Road Less Traveled	6361	Rules Are Made To Be Broken
6325	Road To Hell Is Paved On All Sides With Good Intentions		
		6362	Run A Tight Ship
		6363	Run Amuck
6326	Roaring Fire	6364	Run Circles Around
6327	Rob Peter To Pay Paul	6365	Run For Your Money
6328	Robbing Peter To Pay Paul	6366	Run Into The Ground
6329	Rock & Roll Never Forgets	6367	Run It Up The Flagpole And See Who Salutes It
6330	Rock Around The Clock		
6331	Rock n Roll	6368	Run Like The Wind
6332	Roll Of The Dice		

114

6369	Run The Gamut
6370	Run The Gauntlet
6371	Run With The Fox And Bark With The Hounds
6372	Runnin' With The Devil
6373	Running Around Like A Chicken With It's Head Cut Off
6374	Running On Empty
6375	Running On Faith
6376	Running With Wolves
6377	Runs Like A Top
6378	Sacred Cow
6379	Saddled With Work
6380	Safety First
6381	Sail Into The Sunset
6382	Sailing Under False Colors
6383	Saint Elmo's Fire
6384	Sake It To Me Baby
6385	Salt Of The Earth
6386	Same Bat Time Same Bat Channel
6387	Same Ol' Same Ol'
6388	Same Old Song And Dance
6389	Santa Claus Is Coming To Town
6390	Saturday Night Live
6391	Save By The Bell
6392	Save For A Rainy Day
6393	Save The Drama For Your Mama
6394	Save Up All Your Tears
6395	Save Us From Our Friends
6396	Save Us The Aisle Seats
6397	Save Your Breath
6398	Save Your Own Nest Egg
6399	Saved By The Bell
6400	Saving Face
6401	Savvy Investor
6402	Sawing A Log
6403	Say Good Night Gracie

6404	Say Hello To My Little Friend
6405	Say It Isn't So
6406	Say Uncle
6407	Say What
6408	Say What You Will
6409	Say Yer Prayers Rabbit
6410	Say Your Prayers
6411	Scalawag
6412	Scarce As Hen's Teeth
6413	Scare Crow
6414	Scare The Daylights Out Of You
6415	Scared Dogs Bark Most
6416	Scared Of His Own Shadow
6417	Scared Stiff
6418	Scaredy Cat
6419	Scattered To The Four Winds
6420	School Days
6421	School's Out
6422	Scot Free
6423	Scrabble Eggs Can't Be Unscrambled
6424	Scraping The Bottom Of The Barrel
6425	Scratch And Dent
6426	Scratch My Back And I'll Scratch Yours
6427	Screaming Bloody Murder
6428	Screaming Mimi
6429	Screw It
6430	Sea Change
6431	Seal The Deal
6432	Second Banana
6433	Second Time Around
6434	Second To None
6435	Second Wind
6436	See A Penny Pick It Up All The Day You'll Have Good Luck
6437	See Eye To Eye

115

6438	See No Evil Hear No Evil Speak No Evil
6439	See The Glass As Half Full Or Half Empty
6440	See The Light
6441	See The Whole Board
6442	See The Whole Field
6443	See The World Through Rose Colored Glasses
6444	See What I've Got Lined Up
6445	See Which Way The Wind Blows
6446	See You Later Alligator
6447	Seeing Is Believing
6448	Seeing Red
6449	Seek And Ye Shall Find
6450	Seek To Achieve
6451	Seems Just Like Old Times
6452	See's The Glass As Half Full
6453	Seize The Day
6454	Seize The Days Boys Make Your Lives Extraordinary
6455	Seize The Moment
6456	Self Preservation Is The First Rule Of Nature
6457	Sell Out
6458	Senator- You're No Jack Kennedy
6459	Send It Back
6460	Send It To Them Again
6461	Send Up A Trial Balloon
6462	Sensory Overload
6463	Sent To The Coventry
6464	Separate The Men From The Boys
6465	Separate The Wheat From The Chaff
6466	Serendipity
6467	Serve Up A Fat Pitch
6468	Serve Up A Lollipop

6469	Serve Up A Softball
6470	Set It An Forget It
6471	Set One's Teeth On Edge
6472	Set The Record Straight
6473	Set The Table
6474	Set Your Cap
6475	Set Your Teeth On Edge
6476	Seven Year Itch
6477	Sex Drugs And Rock n Roll
6478	Shake A Stick At
6479	Shake Down
6480	Shake Hands With The Wife's Best Friend
6481	Shake That Thing
6482	Shake The Cobwebs Out
6483	Shake Your Booty
6484	Shaken But Not Stirred
6485	Shangri La
6486	Shape Up Or Ship Out
6487	Sharp As A Marble
6488	Sharp As A Sack Of Wet Mice
6489	Sharp As A Tack
6490	She Could Test The Patience Of Job
6491	She Drinks Like A Fish
6492	She Drives Me Crazy
6493	She Fell Out Of The Ugly Tree
6494	She Gave Me A Withering Glance
6495	She Goes Through Money Like A Fart Through A Pair Of Jeans
6496	She Got Called Up On The Carpet
6497	She Has A Great Personality
6498	She Has A Green Thumb
6499	She Has Bats In Her Belfry
6500	She Has Clout

116

6501	She Has Everything But The Kitchen Sink
6502	She Has The Personality Of A Dead Fish
6503	She Is A Loose Cannon
6504	She Ran The Gamut Of Emotions From A To B
6505	She Threw A Wet Blanket On My Idea
6506	She Wears Her Heart On Her Sleeve
6507	She Wouldn't Know Me From Adam
6508	Shed Some Light
6509	Shed Some Light On It
6510	She'll Be Right
6511	Shell Shocked
6512	Shenanigan
6513	She's A Material Girl
6514	She's A Peach
6515	She's A Super Model You Know
6516	She's All That And More
6517	She's All Twitter Pated
6518	She's An Open Book
6519	She's Been Hit With An Ugly Stick
6520	She's Burning Her Candle At Both Ends
6521	She's Fighting A Losing Battle
6522	She's Getting The Red Carpet Treatment
6523	She's Got Eye's In The Back Of Her Head
6524	She's Got Money To Burn
6525	She's Hot To Trot
6526	She's In Hot Water
6527	She's Lost Her Marbles
6528	She's Not The Brightest Bulb On The Patio
6529	She's Not The Only Fish In The Sea
6530	She's Out Sowing Her Wild Oats
6531	She's Out To Lunch
6532	She's Taking The Bait
6533	She's Tugging On Your Chain
6534	Ship Shape
6535	Ships That Pass In The Night
6536	Shirley Be
6537	Shirt Off His Back
6538	Shirty Be
6539	Shit Eating Grin
6540	Shit Happens
6541	Shit Or Get Off The Pot
6542	Shit Out Of Luck
6543	Shiver Me Timber
6544	Shoe In
6545	Shoe Is On The Other Foot
6546	Shoestring Budget
6547	Shoot First And Ask Questions Later
6548	Shoot From The Hip
6549	Shoot It Straight
6550	Shoot Straight
6551	Shoot The Breeze
6552	Shoot The Bull
6553	Shoot The Rock
6554	Shoot Yourself In The Foot
6555	Shooting Ducks Left And Right
6556	Shooting Fish In A Barrel
6557	Shooting For The Moon
6558	Shop Talk
6559	Shop Till You Drop
6560	Short Changed
6561	Short End Of The Stick
6562	Short Fuse

6563	Short Pleasures Are Often Long Regretted
6564	Shot Across The Bow
6565	Shot In The Arm
6566	Shot In The Dark
6567	Shot The Bull
6568	Shotgun Approach
6569	Shotgun Wedding
6570	Should I Stay
6571	Shouldn't Look Down On It
6572	Shove Off
6573	Show And Tell
6574	Show Him The Door
6575	Show Me The Money
6576	Show Some Backbone
6577	Show Some Spine
6578	Show Some Spunk
6579	Show Them How The Cow Ate The Cabbage
6580	Showing You The Ropes
6581	Shuffle Off This Mortal Coil
6582	Shut Out
6583	Shut The Hole In Your Head
6584	Shut Up
6585	Shut Up And Drive
6586	Shut Your Hole
6587	Shut Your Mouth
6588	Sick And Tired
6589	Sick As A Dog
6590	Sick To Death Of It
6591	Sign On The Dotted Line
6592	Signed Sealed And Delivered
6593	Silence Is Golden
6594	Silenced The Crowd
6595	Silly Rabbit Trix Are For Kids
6596	Simon Says
6597	Simple Kind Of Life
6598	Simple Pleasure Are The Best

6599	Sin City
6600	Since You've Been Gone
6601	Sing A Different Tune
6602	Sing A Few Lines Of Old Woop Dee Doo
6603	Sing For Your Supper
6604	Sing Like A Bird
6605	Sink Or Swim
6606	Sink Your Teeth Into It
6607	Sit Tight
6608	Sitting Duck
6609	Sitting In The Catbird Seat
6610	Sitting On Pins And Needles
6611	Sitting On The Fence
6612	Six And One And A Half Dozen Of Another
6613	Six Feet Under
6614	Six Of One And Half A Dozen Of The Other
6615	Sixty Four Million Dollar Question
6616	Skating On Thin Ice
6617	Skedaddle
6618	Skeletons In The Closet
6619	Skin Flint
6620	Skin The Cat
6621	Sky's The Limit
6622	Slam Dunk
6623	Slap On The Back
6624	Sleep Like A Baby
6625	Sleep Like A Log
6626	Sleep Tight
6627	Sleep With The Fishes
6628	Sleeping Her Way To The Top
6629	Sleeping Like A Baby
6630	Sliced Just The Way You Like It
6631	Slick As Snot On A Glass Doorknob

6632	Slicker Than Gooey Boogers On A Door Knob
6633	Slim To None
6634	Slip A Mickey Finn
6635	Slip Of The Tongue
6636	Slip Shod
6637	Slipped Through Your Fingers
6638	Slippery As An Eel
6639	Slippery Slope
6640	Sloppy As A Soup Sandwich
6641	Sloshed
6642	Slow And Steady Wins The Race
6643	Slow As A Week
6644	Slow As A Wet Work Week
6645	Slow As Molasses In January
6646	Slow But Sure
6647	Slow Down
6648	Slower Than A Seven-Year Itch
6649	Sly As A Fox
6650	Smack Dab In The Middle
6651	Small Fry
6652	Small Potatoes
6653	Small World Isn't It
6654	Smart Ass
6655	Smart Cookies Don't Crumble
6656	Smart Is Better Than Stupid
6657	Smarter Than The Average Bear
6658	Smashed
6659	Smell A Little Ripe To You
6660	Smells A Little Ripe
6661	Smile And The World Smiles With You Cry And You Cry Alone
6662	Smile You're On Candid Camera

6663	Smoke And Mirrors
6664	Smoking Gun
6665	Smooth As A Baby's Bottom
6666	Smooth Operator
6667	Smooth Over
6668	Snafu
6669	Snail's Pace
6670	Snake Eyes
6671	Snake In The Grass
6672	Snap Out Of It
6673	Sneakers Up
6674	Snockered
6675	Snow Job
6676	Snowball's Chance In Hell
6677	Snug As A Bug In A Rug
6678	So Be It
6679	So Close Can Taste It
6680	So Close You Can Taste It
6681	So Easy A Child Could Do It
6682	So Far So Good
6683	So Fast Your Head Will Spin
6684	So Head On Over
6685	So Help Me God
6686	So Many Men So Little Time
6687	So Much Bad In The Best Of Us And So Much Good In The Worst In Us
6688	So Much For That
6689	So Quiet You Could Hear A Pin Drop
6690	So Ugly They'd Have To Sneak Up On A Glass Of Water To Get A Drink
6691	So What
6692	So What Do You Do
6693	So What's The Catch
6694	Soccer Punches
6695	Sock It To Me
6696	Sod Off

119

6697	Soda Jerk	6722	Sooner Or Later
6698	Sold Down The River	6723	Sooth Sayer
6699	Sold Out	6724	Sorry Charlie
6700	Solid As A Rock	6725	Sound Like A Broken Record
6701	Some Animals Are More Equal Than Others	6726	Sounding Off
6702	Some Pots You Don't Stir	6727	Sounds Like A Plan
6703	Some Things Are Better Left Unsaid	6728	Sounds Too Good To Be True
		6729	Soup To Nuts
6704	Some Things Belong On Paper Others In Life	6730	Sour Grapes
6705	Some Things Never Grow Old	6731	South End Of A North-Bound Horse
6706	Someday You Will Thank Me For This	6732	South Paw
		6733	Sow Your Wild Oats
6707	Someday You Will Thank Me For Bringing You Into This World	6734	Space The Final Frontier
		6735	Spaghetti On The Wall
6708	Something Rotten In The State Of Denmark	6736	Spare The Rod Spoil The Child
6709	Something Smells Fishy	6737	Spare The Rod But Don't Spoil The Child
6710	Something To Believe In	6738	Speak Of The Devil
6711	Something You Can Really Sink Your Teeth Into	6739	Speak Off The Cuff
6712	Something's Never Die	6740	Speak Softly And Carry A Big Stick
6713	Sometimes You Are The Hydrant And Sometimes You Are The Dog	6741	Speak To The Hand
		6742	Speak With A Forked Tongue
6714	Sometimes You Are The Windshield And Sometimes You Are The Bug	6743	Speaking In Riddles
		6744	Speaks Volumes About You
6715	Sometimes You Just Gotta Let Your Hair Down	6745	Specialty Of The House
		6746	Spick And Span
6716	Somewhere Along The Road Their Ship Went Off The Rails	6747	Spill The Dirt
		6748	Spin A Yarn
		6749	Spineless Wimp
6717	Somewhere Over The Rainbow	6750	Spinning Your Wheels
		6751	Spit And Polish
6718	Son Of A Bitch	6752	Spit In One Hand And Wish In The Other
6719	Son Of A Gun	
6720	Song And Dance	6753	Spit The Dummy
6721	Soon Will I Rest	6754	Spitting Image

120

6755	Split Second	6791	Stay Tuned For A Message From Our Sponsor
6756	Splitting Hairs	6792	Stayed Too Long At The Fair
6757	Spoil The Fun	6793	Staying On Top Of It
6758	Spoon Full Of Sugar Helps The Medicine Go Down	6794	Staying Power
6759	Spread The News	6795	Steal My Thunder
6760	Spread The Word	6796	Steal Someone's Thunder
6761	Spreading Like Wildfire	6797	Stealing The Show
6762	Spreading The News	6798	Steer Clear Of It
6763	Spring Is In The Air	6799	Stem The Tide
6764	Spruce Up	6800	Step On A Crack Break Your Mother's Back
6765	Squeaky Wheel Gets The Grease	6801	Step On It
6766	Squeal On	6802	Step Up To The Plate
6767	Stab In The Back	6803	Stepping On People's Toes
6768	Stack The Deck	6804	Stew In One's Own Juice
6769	Stake Your Claim	6805	Stick A Fork In It
6770	Stand Down	6806	Stick A Sock In It
6771	Stand On Your Own Two Feet	6807	Stick It In Your Ear
6772	Stand Out From The Crowd	6808	Stick It Out
6773	Stand Pat	6809	Stick It To You
6774	Stand The Test Of Time	6810	Stick It Where The Sun Don't Shine
6775	Stand Up And Be Counted	6811	Stick One's Neck Out
6776	Stand Up Straight	6812	Stick To Your Guns
6777	Stand Your Ground	6813	Stick Up For The Little Guy
6778	Standing On The Shoulder's Of Giants	6814	Stick With It
6779	Staring Off Into Space	6815	Stick Your Neck Out
6780	Start Spreading The News	6816	Sticks And Stones Will Break My Bones But Words Will Never Hurt Me
6781	Start The Day Off Right	6817	Sticks Out Like A Sore Thumb
6782	Start Your Engines	6818	Sticky Subject
6783	Starting From Scratch	6819	Stiff As A Board
6784	Starting Over Again	6820	Stiff Neck
6785	State Of The Art	6821	Stiff Upper Lip
6786	Stay In The Game	6822	Stifle
6787	Stay In The Loop	6823	Still As A Church Mouse
6788	Stay On Your Own Side		
6789	Stay Out Of The Water		
6790	Stay Tuned		

121

6824	Still Waters Run Deep	6859	Strictly For The Birds
6825	Stink To High Heaven	6860	Strike A Bargain
6826	Stinks To The Highest Heaven	6861	Strike While The Irons Hot
6827	Stinks To High Heaven	6862	String Him Along
6828	Stir Up An Ant's Nest	6863	Stripped To The Bone
6829	Stirring Up Trouble	6864	Strong As An Ox
6830	Stitch In Time Saves Nine	6865	Struck My Funny Bone
6831	Stolen Waters Are Sweet	6866	Stubborn As A Mule
6832	Stone Faced	6867	Stuck In A Rut
6833	Stone The Crows	6868	Stuck Out Like A Sore Thumb
6834	Stone Walls Does Not A Prison Make	6869	Stuck Up Be
6835	Stoned	6870	Stuffed Shirt
6836	Stone's Throw Away	6871	Stupid Is As Stupid Does
6837	Stood Out Like A Sore Tooth	6872	Success Breeds Success
6838	Stool Pigeon	6873	Success Has A Thousand Fathers While Failure Is An Orphan
6839	Stop And Smell The Roses	6874	Success Isn't For The Timid
6840	Stop Gap	6875	Such A Deal
6841	Stop He's Headed For The Barn	6876	Suck It Up
6842	Stop Him Dead	6877	Suck Up
6843	Stop Him For He's Headed For The Barn	6878	Sucker
6844	Stop In The Name Of Love	6879	Suffice It To Say
6845	Stop On A Dime	6880	Sugar In His Shorts
6846	Stop The Presses	6881	Sugarcoat Something
6847	Stop Them In Their Tracks	6882	Suit Up
6848	Stopped In Her Tracks	6883	Super Duper
6849	Stow It Down	6884	Survival Of The Fittest
6850	Straight Arrow	6885	Swallow Hook Line And Sinker
6851	Straight From The Horse's Mouth	6886	Swallow One's Pride
6852	Straight Laced	6887	Swan Song
6853	Straight Up	6888	Swap Forces In Midstream
6854	Straighten Up And Fly Right	6889	Swash Buckler
6855	Stranger In A Strange Land	6890	Swear On The Bible
6856	Strapped For Cash	6891	Sweat Blood
6857	Stress Out	6892	Sweat Equity
6858	Stretch A Dollar	6893	Sweat The Details
		6894	Sweating Blood

6895	Sweating Bullets	6930	Take A Rain Check
6896	Sweating Like A Pig	6931	Take A Small Leap Of Faith
6897	Sweep It Under The Rug	6932	Take A Step Back
6898	Sweet 16 And Never Been Kissed	6933	Take A Step Forward
		6934	Take A Test Drive
6899	Sweet As Sugar	6935	Take Aback
6900	Sweet Deal	6936	Take Care Of Your Knitting
6901	Sweet Sixteen	6937	Take Five
6902	Sweeten The Pot	6938	Take For A Ride
6903	Sweetheart Deal	6939	Take Him To Task
6904	Swim Against The Tide	6940	Take It And Run With It
6905	Swim Up Stream	6941	Take It At Face Value
6906	Swim With The Sharks	6942	Take It Easy
6907	Swimming In Molasses	6943	Take It From Me
		6944	Take It Like A Man
6908	Ta Dah	6945	Take It Lying Down
6909	Tackle My Homework	6946	Take It On The Lam
6910	Tail Between His Legs	6947	Take It Or Leave It
6911	Take A Back Seat	6948	Take It To The Bank
6912	Take A Back Seat To	6949	Take It To The Limit
6913	Take A Bath	6950	Take It With A Grain Of Salt
6914	Take A Bow	6951	Take My Breath Away
6915	Take A Break	6952	Take My Wife Please
6916	Take A Breather	6953	Take My Word For It
6917	Take A Chill Pill	6954	Take No Prisoners
6918	Take A Dump	6955	Take One For The Team
6919	Take A Haircut	6956	Take Stock Of
6920	Take A Hike	6957	Take That Leap Of Faith
6921	Take A Leaf Out Of Your Book	6958	Take That To The Bank And Smoke It
6922	Take A Leak	6959	Take The Bitter With The Sweet
6923	Take A Long Walk Off A Short Pier	6960	Take The Bull By The Horns
6924	Take A Long Walk Off A Short Plank	6961	Take The Crowd Out Of The Game
6925	Take A Look Around	6962	Take The Day Off
6926	Take A Look At This	6963	Take The Easy Way Out
6927	Take A Picture It Will Last Longer	6964	Take The Gloves Off
6928	Take A Position	6965	Take The Good With The Bad
6929	Take A Powder		

123

6966	Take The Money And Run	7000	Talking Gibberish
6967	Take The Plunge	7001	Talking Out Of Your Head
6968	Take The Wind Out Of Your Sail	7002	Talking Through Your Hat
6969	Take The World By Storm	7003	Talking To Ralph On The Big White Telephone
6970	Take This Job And Shove It	7004	Talking Turkey
6971	Take To The Tall Timber	7005	Tall Dark And Handsome
6972	Take Under One's Wing	7006	Tall Tale
6973	Take You Down A Peg	7007	Taming The Tide
6974	Take Your Fate Into Your Own Hands	7008	Tan Your Hide
		7009	Tanked
6975	Take Your Life In Your Own Hands	7010	Tantamount
		7011	Tarred And Feathered
6976	Taken By Storm	7012	Taste Of Your Own Medicine
6977	Taken Down A Peg	7013	Tastes Great Less Filling
6978	Taken For A Ride	7014	Tattle Tale
6979	Taken To The Cleaners	7015	Teach A Man How To Fish And You'll Feed Him For Life
6980	Taken With A Grain Of Salt		
6981	Takes All The Guess Work Out Of It	7016	Teacher's Pet
		7017	Team Player
6982	Takes Its Toll On You	7018	Tear Into It
6983	Takes The Cake	7019	Tear You A New Asshole
6984	Takin' Care Of Business	7020	Technicolor Yawn
6985	Taking A Back Seat	7021	Technicolor Yawn The
6986	Taking A Chance On Love	7022	Technology No Place For Wimps
6987	Taking His Pound Of Flesh		
6988	Taking The Easy Way Out	7023	Tee Totaller
6989	Taking The Scenic Route	7024	Tell It To Me Straight
6990	Taking The World By Storm	7025	Tell Me About It
6991	Talk A Blue Streak	7026	Tell Me About It Stud
6992	Talk Is Cheap	7027	Tell Me What You Don't Like About Yourself
6993	Talk Of The Devil And He Is Bound To Appear		
		7028	Tell Tail
6994	Talk Shop	7029	Tell That To The Marines
6995	Talk The Talk And Walk The Walk	7030	Tell The Truth And Shame The Devil
		7031	Tell Your Story Walking
6996	Talk To The Hand	7032	Tell-A-Porta Potty
6997	Talk Until You Are Blue In The Face	7033	Tempest In A Teapot
6998	Talkin' Trash		
6999	Talking Behind His Back		

124

7034	Ten To One
7035	Tend The Garden
7036	Tender Foot
7037	Test The Waters
7038	Testing One's Mettle
7039	Tetched In The Head
7040	TGIF
7041	Thank God It's Friday
7042	Thank Goodness
7043	Thank Goodness It's Friday
7044	Thank Goodness You're Alive
7045	Thank Heaven For Little Girls
7046	Thank Your Lucky Stars
7047	Thanks A Lot
7048	Thanks But No Thanks
7049	That And A Quarter Will Get You A Cup Of Coffee
7050	That Argument Doesn't Hold Water
7051	That Baby Runs Like A Scalded Dog
7052	That Burns Me Up
7053	That Chaps My Hide
7054	That Doesn't Ring A Bell
7055	That Dog Won't Hunt
7056	That Gets My Goad
7057	That Government Is Best Which Governs Least
7058	That Hits The Spot
7059	That Oughta Tide You Over
7060	That Really Brings It Home
7061	That Sucks
7062	That Takes The Cake
7063	That Was An Eye Opener
7064	That Was Cold Blooded
7065	That Was Like Pulling Hen's Teeth
7066	That Which Does Not Kill You Makes You Stronger
7067	That's The V
7068	That's The
7069	That's What F For
7070	That'll Be Th
7071	That'll Do Pig Tl
7072	That's A Doc
7073	That's A Fact O
7074	That's A Gimm
7075	That's A Joke
7076	That's A Load Off My
7077	That's A Real Stem W
7078	That's A Real Step Forw Into The Unknown
7079	That's A Wrap
7080	That's About The Size Of
7081	That's All Folks
7082	That's All I Have To Give
7083	That's All She Wrote
7084	That's All There Is To It
7085	That's All Well And Good
7086	That's Bogus
7087	That's Cool
7088	That's Debatable
7089	That's Easy For You To Say
7090	That's Enough To Piss Off The Pope
7091	That's For The Birds
7092	That's Hot
7093	That's How The Cow Eats The Cabbage
7094	That's Icing On The Cake
7095	That's It In A Nutshell
7096	That's Just Cheesy
7097	That's Just Like The Pot Calling The Kettle Black
7098	That's Just Peachy
7099	That's Just The Tip Of The Iceberg
7100	That's Killing The Cat With Two Stones

7101	That's Life
7102	That's Like A Turtle On A Fence Post
7103	That's Music To My Ears
7104	That's No Joke
7105	That's No Skin Off My Nose
7106	That's Old Hat
7107	That's One Small Step For Man One Giant Leap For Mankind
7108	That's Par For The Course
7109	That's Pretty Run Of The Mill
7110	That's Right Zuzu Atta Boy Clarence
7111	That's Rubber On The Side Of The Road
7112	That's Show Business
7113	That's Skull Duggery
7114	That's Some Ole Good
7115	That's Such A Cliche
7116	That's That
7117	That's That Way It Is
7118	That's The $64,000 Question
7119	That's The Bomb
7120	That's The Icing On The Camel's Back
7121	That's The Long And Short Of It
7122	That's The Name Of The Game
7123	That's The Sixty Four Thousand Dollar Question
7124	That's The Ticket
7125	That's The Way It Was
7126	That's The Way Lady Luck Dances
7127	That's The Way The Ball Bounces
7128	That's The Way The Cookie Crumbles

7129	That's The Way The Mop Flops
7130	That's The Whole Ball Of Wax
7131	That's Too Close For Comfort
7132	That's Water Over The Damn
7133	That's Water Under The Bridge
7134	That's Where I Draw The Line
7135	That's Where The Money Is
7136	The Lesser Of Two Evils
7137	The Acorn Doesn't Fall Far From The Tree
7138	The Agony Of Defeat
7139	The Answer To Their Prayers
7140	The Ball Is In Your Court
7141	The Beat Goes On
7142	The Bee's Knees
7143	The Belle Of The Ball
7144	The Best Cure For Insomnia Is To Get A Lot Of Sleep
7145	The Best Is Yet To Come
7146	The Best Of Both Worlds
7147	The Best Thing Since Little Apples
7148	The Best Things In Life Are Free
7149	The Big Apple
7150	The Big Cheese
7151	The Big Picture
7152	The Bigger The Better
7153	The Bigger They Are The Harder They Fall
7154	The Blind Leading The Blind
7155	The Bloom Is Off The Rose
7156	The Body Is Still Warm
7157	The Bomb

7158	The Bottom Fell Out
7159	The Bottom Line
7160	The Boys Are Back In Town
7161	The Brush Off
7162	The Buck Stops Here
7163	The Bullfrog's Beard
7164	The Butler Did It
7165	The Calm Before The Storm
7166	The Cat's Meow
7167	The Cat's Out Of The Bag
7168	The Cat's Pajamas
7169	The Chains That Bind
7170	The Circle Of Life
7171	The Clam's Garters
7172	The Clock Is Ticking
7173	The Cream Of The Crop
7174	The Cuckoo's Chin
7175	The Darkest Hour Is Just Before Dawn
7176	The Devil Is Always Ready To Rock The Cradle Of The Saint Who Sleeps
7177	The Devil Is In The Details
7178	The Devil Made Me Do It
7179	The Devil Must Be Beating His Wife
7180	The Discerning Eye Is A Pain In The Neck
7181	The Dog Ate My Homework
7182	The Dogs Bollocks
7183	The Duck's Quack
7184	The Early Bird Catches The Worm
7185	The Eel's Ankles
7186	The Eight Hundred Pound Gorilla
7187	The Elephant's Arches
7188	The Elephant's Wrist
7189	The Emperor Has No Clothes
7190	The End

	Justifies The Means
7191	The Enemy Of My Enemy Is My Friend
7192	The Everyman
7193	The Exception That Proves The Rule
7194	The Exception To The Rule
7195	The Eye Of The Tiger
7196	The Eyes Are Bigger Than The Stomach
7197	The Eyes Are The Windows To The Soul
7198	The Fact Of The Matter Is
7199	The Fair Haired One
7200	The Fall Guy
7201	The Fickle Finger Of Fate
7202	The Final Nail In The Coffin
7203	The Full Monty
7204	The Fur Flying
7205	The Future Ain't What It Used To Be
7206	The Game Is On The Line
7207	The Genie Is Out Of The Bottle
7208	The Girl Next Door
7209	The Glass Of The Mirror Simply Melted Away
7210	The Gloves Are Off
7211	The Gnat's Elbow
7212	The Golden Child
7213	The Golden Nugget
7214	The Good The Bad The Ugly
7215	The Gospel Truth
7216	The Grass Is Always Greener On The Other Side
7217	The Great Pretender
7218	The Greatest Gift Of All
7219	The Greatest Love Of All
7220	The Greatest Thing Since Sliced Bread

127

7221	The Hand That Rocks The Cradle	7249	The Meek Shall Inherit The Earth
7222	The Handwriting Is On The Wall	7250	The Melting Pot
7223	The Hostess With The Mostess	7251	The Moment Of Truth
7224	The Hot Seat	7252	The More The Merrier
7225	The Human Experience	7253	The More Things Change The More They Stay The Same
7226	The Icing On The Cake	7254	The More We Learn The Less We Know
7227	The King Can Do No Wrong	7255	The Mother Of All Inventions
7228	The Lady Is A Tramp	7256	The Mountain Labored And Brought Forth A Mouse
7229	The Land Was Ours Before We Were The Land	7257	The Nail That Sticks Up Gets Hammered Down
7230	The Last Hurrah	7258	The Nail That Sticks Up Gets Pounded Down
7231	The Last Straw	7259	The New Media Is The New Math
7232	The Leopard's Stripes	7260	The New Norm
7233	The Life Of Riley	7261	The Night Is Young And So Are We
7234	The Lights Are On But There's Nobody Home	7262	The Old Ball And Chain
7235	The Lion Shall Lie Down With The Lamb	7263	The One And Only
7236	The Lion's Den	7264	The One That Got Away
7237	The Lion's Share	7265	The Only Difference Between Women And Girls Is The Price Of Their Pearls
7238	The Long & Winding Road	7266	The Only People I Trust Are You And Me And I Am Not Too Sure About You
7239	The Long And Short Of It	7267	The Only Thing We Have To Fear Is Fear Itself
7240	The Long Arm Of The Law	7268	The Operation Was Successful But The Patient Died
7241	The Lord Giveth And The Lord Taketh Away	7269	The Oxen Are Slow But The Earth Is Patient
7242	The Lord Moves In Mysterious Ways	7270	The Party's Over
7243	The Love Of Money Is The Root Of All Evil	7271	The Path Of Least Resistance
7244	The Lowest On The Totem Pole		
7245	The Luck Of The Draw		
7246	The Luck Stops Here		
7247	The Main Dish		
7248	The Man In The Street		

128

7272	The Pen Is Mightier Than The Sword
7273	The Peter Principle
7274	The Phoenix Is Rising
7275	The Pick Of The Litter
7276	The Picture Of Health
7277	The Pig's Wings
7278	The Place Was Crawling With Cops
7279	The Plain And Utter Truth
7280	The Pot Calling The Kettle Black
7281	The Pot Of Gold At The End Of The Rainbow
7282	The Power Of Prayer
7283	The Project At Hand
7284	The Proof Is In The Pudding
7285	The Proof Of The Pudding Is In The Eating
7286	The Quiet Before The Storm
7287	The Raw End Of The Deal
7288	The Real Deal
7289	The Real McCoy
7290	The Rest Is History
7291	The Rich Get Richer And The Poor Get Poorer
7292	The Rising Tide Lifts All Boats
7293	The Risk Of Loss
7294	The Road Less Traveled
7295	The Road To Hell Is Paved With Good Intentions
7296	The Road To Ruin Is Paved With Good Intentions
7297	The Rock Of Gibraltar
7298	The Roll Of The Dice
7299	The Sardine's Whiskers
7300	The Second Time Around
7301	The Seven Year Itch
7302	The Shit Hits The Fan
7303	The Shoe Is On The Other Foot
7304	The Shoemaker's Kids Always Go Barefoot
7305	The Shoes Are On The Other Foot Now
7306	The Short End Of The Stick
7307	The Shot Heard Around The World
7308	The Show Must Go On
7309	The Sincerest Form Of Flattery
7310	The Sky Is Not Going To Fall
7311	The Sky's The Limit
7312	The Snake's Hips
7313	The Sooner The Better
7314	The Sound Of Silence Is Deafening
7315	The Spirit Is Willing But The Flesh Is Weak
7316	The Spring Ritual
7317	The Squeaky Wheel Gets The Grease
7318	The Straw That Broke The Camel's Back
7319	The Stronger The Breeze The Stronger The Trees
7320	The Strongest Steel Is Cast In The Hottest Fire
7321	The Strongest Winds Blow On The Highest Mountains
7322	The Stuff That Dreams Are Made Of
7323	The Supernatural Is The Natural Not Yet Understood
7324	The Tables Are Turned
7325	The Tail That Wagged The Dog
7326	The Tale Of The Tape

129

7327	The Third Time Is The Charm
7328	The Thrill Of Victory The Agony Of Defeat
7329	The Thunder Rolls
7330	The Tide Is High
7331	The Tide Waits For No One
7332	The Tide's Beginning To Turn
7333	The Tiger's Spots
7334	The Time Of Your Life
7335	The Times They Are A Changing
7336	The Torch Has Been Passed To A New Generation
7337	The Tower Of Babel
7338	The Tribe Has Spoken
7339	The Truth Hurts
7340	The Truth Is Out There
7341	The Truth Often Hurts
7342	The Truth Shall Make You Free
7343	The Truth The Whole Truth And Nothing But The Truth
7344	The Twilight Years
7345	The UFO's Is How Our Worst Fears Were Groundless
7346	The Unabridged Version
7347	The Universe Is Conspiring In My Favor
7348	The Voice Of The People Is The Voice Of God
7349	The Walls Have Ears
7350	The Walls Start Closing
7351	The Way To A Man's Heart Is Through His Stomach
7352	The Wheel Comes Full Circle
7353	The Whole Ball Of Wax
7354	The Whole Enchilada

7355	The Whole Kit And Kaboodle
7356	The Whole Nine Yards
7357	The Whole Shootin' Match
7358	The Wind Beneath My Wings
7359	The Winter Of Our Discontent
7360	The Wisdom Of Solomon
7361	The Wolf Is At The Door
7362	The Word Is The Word
7363	The Word On The Street
7364	The World Is Not Flat
7365	The World Is Your Oyster
7366	The Wrong Side Of The Tracks
7367	Their Ace
7368	Their Ace In The Hole
7369	Their Name Is Legion
7370	Them's Fightin' Words
7371	There Are Lies Damned Lies And Statistics
7372	There Are None So Blind As Those Will Not See
7373	There Are Other Fish In The Sea
7374	There Are Starving Children In Africa
7375	There Are Two Sides To Every Story
7376	There But For The Grace Of God Go I
7377	There For The Taking
7378	There Is A God
7379	There Is Honor Even Among Thieves
7380	There Is More Than One Way To Skin A Cat
7381	There Is No "I" In Team
7382	There Is No Cow On The Ice
7383	There Is No I In Team

7384	There Is No Time Like The Present
7385	There Isn't A Mean Bone Is His Body
7386	There Lies The Rub
7387	There Now That Wasn't So Bad Was It
7388	There Ought To Be A Law Against That
7389	There Was Never A Dull Moment
7390	There You Go Again
7391	There's No Business Like Show Business
7392	There's Your Trouble
7393	There'll Be Hell To Pay
7394	There'll Never Be Another You
7395	There's A First Time For Everything
7396	There's A Fly In My Soup
7397	There's A God And I'm Not Him
7398	There's A Pot Of Gold At The End Of A Rainbow
7399	There's A Season And A Time For Every Purpose Under Heaven
7400	There's A Skeleton In Every Closet
7401	There's A Snake In My Boot
7402	There's A Sucker Born Every Minute
7403	There's A Time And Place For Everything
7404	There's A Time To Be Born And A Time To Die
7405	There's Always A Light At The End Of The Tunnel
7406	There's Always A Reason For What Happens

7407	There's Always Room At The Top
7408	There's Always Tomorrow
7409	There's An Exception To Every Rule
7410	There's Going To Be Hell To Pay
7411	There's Gold In Them Thar Hills
7412	There's Good And Bad In Everything
7413	There's Many A Slip Between Cup And Lip
7414	There's More Than One Way To Skin A Cat
7415	There's More To It Than Meets The Eye
7416	There's More Where That Came From
7417	There's No Accounting For Tastes
7418	There's No Business Like Show Business
7419	There's No Crying In Baseball
7420	There's No Fool Like An Old Fool
7421	There's No Joy In Mudville
7422	There's No Place Like Home
7423	There's No Royal Road To Learning
7424	There's No Substitute For Victory
7425	There's No Such Thing As A Free Lunch
7426	There's No Such Thing As A Free Ride
7427	There's No Time Like The Present
7428	There's No Try
7429	There's No Turning Back

7430	There's No Wrath Like A Women's Scorn
7431	There's Nothing Good Or Bad But Thinking Makes It So
7432	There's Nothing New Under The Sun
7433	There's One In Every Crowd
7434	There's Safety In Numbers
7435	There's Something Fishy About That
7436	There's Something Fishy In The State Of Denmark
7437	There's Something I've Been Meaning To Tell You
7438	There's Still A Few Voters Undecided
7439	These Are The Times
7440	These Boots Are Made For Walkin'
7441	They Call Me Mr. Tibbs
7442	They Can't Buy A Run
7443	They Can't Take That Away From Me
7444	They Died With Their Boots On
7445	They Don't Write 'Em Like That Anymore
7446	They Gave Him Carte Blanche
7447	They Have Got Their Feet On The Ground
7448	They Have Missed So Many Chances They Must Be Wringing Their Heads In Shame
7449	They Need To Take Care Of The Rock
7450	They Never Miss An Opportunity To Miss An Opportunity

7451	They Play Good "D"
7452	They That Sow The Wind Shall Reap The Whirlwind
7453	They Threw The Book At Him
7454	They We're Young And Beautiful
7455	They'll Never Know What Hit Them
7456	They're A Dime A Dozen
7457	They're Called Boobs Ed
7458	They're Getting Hitched
7459	They're Here
7460	They're Jumping The Broomstick
7461	They're Like Two Peas In A Pod
7462	They're Puppets On A String
7463	They've Been Playing You Like A Fiddle
7464	Thick As A Brick
7465	Thick As A Ditch
7466	Thick As Pea Soup
7467	Thick Headed
7468	Thin As Six O'Clock
7469	Thing Is
7470	Thingamajig
7471	Things Are About To Get Serious
7472	Things Are Not Always As They Seem
7473	Things Aren't What They Used To Be
7474	Think Before You Speak
7475	Think Like A Man
7476	Think Like A Man Act Like A Woman
7477	Think Outside The Box
7478	Think Twice

7479	Thinking With The Wrong Head
7480	Third Degree
7481	Third Times A Charm
7482	Third Time's A Charm The
7483	Third Wheel
7484	Thirty Pieces Of Silver
7485	Thirty Thousand Foot Level
7486	This Alone Is Worth The Price Of Admission
7487	This Could Be The Start Of Something Big
7488	This Could Take All Night
7489	This Hurts Me Worse Than It Does You
7490	This I Promise You
7491	This I Promised You
7492	This Is A Historical Moment
7493	This Is All I Ask
7494	This Is For The Birds
7495	This Is Generally Useful But Not Especially
7496	This Is Going To Hurt You More Than Me
7497	This Is It
7498	This Is The Beginning Of A Beautiful Friendship
7499	This Is The City
7500	This Is The End The Absolute End
7501	This Is The Last Straw
7502	This Is War
7503	This Is What You've Been Waiting For
7504	This Land Is Your Land
7505	This Man's Work Cannot Be Underrated
7506	This Means War
7507	This Moment In Time
7508	This Offer Is Still On The Table
7509	This Old House
7510	This Really Bugs Me
7511	This Time Around
7512	This Time The Dream's On Me
7513	This Too Shall Pass
7514	This Town's Not Big Enough For The Two Of Us
7515	This Way To The Bank
7516	This Will Hurt You More Than It Does Me
7517	Thorn In My Side
7518	Those Who Are Ignorant Offer Their Opinions On Every Subject
7519	Those Who Know Don't Speak Those Who Speak Don't Know
7520	Thought I'd Never See The Day
7521	Three Dog Night
7522	Three Magic Words
7523	Three Sheets To The Wind
7524	Three Squares A Day
7525	Three Strikes And You're Out
7526	Threw A Curve Ball
7527	Threw It With A Little Something On It
7528	Threw Up My Hands In Disgust
7529	Through Rose Colored Glasses
7530	Through Thick And Thin
7531	Throw A Fit
7532	Throw A Monkey Wrench Into The Works
7533	Throw A Steel Wrench In The Works
7534	Throw Caution To The Wind
7535	Throw Cold Water

133

7536	Throw Cold Water On		7570	Till The Cows Come Home
7537	Throw Down		7571	Tilting At Windmills
7538	Throw Dust In Your Eyes		7572	Timber
7539	Throw Gasoline On The Fire		7573	Time After Time
			7574	Time And Again
7540	Throw In The Towel		7575	Time And Tide Waits For No Man
7541	Throw Me A Bone			
7542	Throw The Baby Out With The Bathwater		7576	Time Flies When You're Having Fun
7543	Throw The Book At Him		7577	Time Heals All Wounds
7544	Throw To The Wolves		7578	Time Honored
7545	Throw Your Hat In The Ring		7579	Time Is A Precious Asset And Certainly Not One To Be Wasted
7546	Throwing A Temper Tantrum			
7547	Throwing Aspirin Tablets			
7548	Throwing Caution To The Wind		7580	Time Is Money
			7581	Time Is Of The Essence
7549	Throwing Out The Baby With The Bathwater		7582	Time Is Running Out
			7583	Time Is Short
7550	Throwing Some Fresh Legs On		7584	Time Is Timeless
			7585	Time Is Up
7551	Thumb A Ride		7586	Time Of Your Life
7552	Thumb Your Nose		7587	Time On Your Hands
7553	Thumb Your Nose At		7588	Time Out
7554	Thumbs Down		7589	Time Stands Still
7555	Thumbs Up		7590	Time Tested
7556	Tickle Me Silly		7591	Time To Make The Donuts
7557	Tickle The Ivories		7592	Time To Pay The Piper
7558	Tickled Pink		7593	Time To Play Dirty
7559	Tie The Knot		7594	Time To Turn The Tables
7560	Tied To Your Wife's Apron Strings		7595	Time Waits For No Man
			7596	Time Warp
7561	Tied Up Right Now		7597	Time Will Tell
7562	Tight As A Drum		7598	Time's Change
7563	Tight As The Bark On A Tree		7599	Times They Are A Changing
7564	Tight Wad		7600	Time's Up
7565	Tighten Your Belt		7601	Timing Is Everything
7566	Tighter Than A Drum		7602	Tin Ear
7567	Tighter Than A Gnat's Ass		7603	Tingling With Anticipation
7568	Till Death Do Us Part		7604	Tinhorn Gambler
7569	Till Hell Freezes Over		7605	Tip The Scale

134

7606	Tit For Tat
7607	To Admit Defeat At This Stage Is Slightly Pathetic
7608	To ASSUME Makes An ASS Out Of U And ME
7609	To Be A Piker
7610	To Be Continued
7611	To Be Honest With You
7612	To Be Left Holding The Bag
7613	To Be On Track
7614	To Be Or Not To Be That Is The Question
7615	To Be Tongue Tied
7616	To Beat A Dead Horse
7617	To Blow A Gasket
7618	To Blow Chow
7619	To Blow Chunks
7620	To Bone Up On
7621	To Bounce Back
7622	To Bowl Someone Over
7623	To Break Ranks
7624	To Coin A Phrase
7625	To Cry Wolf
7626	To Die With One's Boots On
7627	To Each His Own
7628	To Err Is Dysfunctional To Forgive Co-Dependent
7629	To Err Is Human To Forgive Devine
7630	To Feather Your Nest
7631	To Go Scot Free
7632	To Go To Pot
7633	To Go To The Dogs
7634	To Have And To Hold
7635	To Have Both Feet Firmly Planted On The Ground
7636	To Have The World On A String
7637	To Have Your Nose In The Air

7638	To Infinity And Beyond
7639	To Jerk Off
7640	To Knock Off
7641	To Lie Down With Lions
7642	To Live From Hand To Mouth
7643	To Make A Long Story Short
7644	To Make Money You Need Money
7645	To Pin Our Hopes On
7646	To Play Second Fiddle
7647	To Protect And Serve
7648	To Put It Mildly
7649	To Ramp Up
7650	To See Eye To Eye
7651	To Tell You The Truth
7652	To The Bitter End
7653	To The Victor Belong The Spoils
7654	To Thine Own Self Be True
7655	To Tie The Knot
7656	To Toy With
7657	To Tread Lightly
7658	To Tune Out
7659	To Wave The White Flag
7660	To Wig Out
7661	Today Is The First Day Of The Rest Of Your Life
7662	Toe The Line
7663	Toe The Mark
7664	Toga Toga
7665	Tom And Jerry
7666	Tom Dick And Harry
7667	Tomorrow Is Another Day
7668	Tomorrow Tomorrow And Another Tomorrow
7669	Tongue And Cheek
7670	Tongue In Cheek
7671	Tongue Lashing

7672	Tongue Tied Be	7704	Toss Your Hat In The Ring
7673	Tonight's The Night	7705	Total Garbage
7674	Too Big For One's Britches	7706	Totally Wasted
7675	Too Little Too Late	7707	Toto I've Got A Feeling We're Not In Kansas Anymore
7676	Too Many Chefs Spoil The Broth	7708	Touch And Go
7677	Too Many Chiefs And Not Enough Indians	7709	Touch Base
7678	Too Many Cooks In The Kitchen	7710	Touch Stone
		7711	Touchy Feelie
7679	Too Many Cooks Spoil The Broth	7712	Tough Luck Sherlock
		7713	Tow The Line
7680	Too Many Cooks Spoil The Soup	7714	Train Of Thought
		7715	Tread Lightly
7681	Too Many Irons In The Fire	7716	Tread Mill
7682	Too Much Information	7717	Treated Like A Dog
7683	Too Much Sail For A Small Craft	7718	Trial By Fire
		7719	Tricks Of The Trade
7684	Too Much Too Little Too Late	7720	Tried And Tested
		7721	Tried And True
7685	Too Rich For My Blood	7722	Trim The Fat
7686	Toodles	7723	Trip Over Your Tongue
7687	Took Me To The Cleaners	7724	Trip The Light Fantastic
7688	Took Off Like A Bat Out Of Hell	7725	Trojan Horse
		7726	Trouble With A Capital `T'
7689	Took Off Like A Shot	7727	Trust Everyone But Cut The Cards
7690	Took Something Off That One	7728	Trust In The Lord And Use Good Equipment
7691	Toot His Own Horn	
7692	Toot Your Own Horn	7729	Truth Is Beauty
7693	Tooth And Nail	7730	Truth Is Stranger Than Fiction
7694	Tooting His Own Horn	
7695	Top Banana	7731	Truth Is Truth To The End Of Reckoning
7696	Top Dog	
7697	Top Of The Food Chain	7732	Truth Lies At The Bottom Of A Well
7698	Top Of The Morning	
7699	Tore Up From The Floor Up	7733	Truth Will Out
7700	Torn Asunder	7734	Try As I Might
7701	Toss Me A Bone	7735	Try To Remember
7702	Toss Me Some Scraps	7736	Try Your Hand At Something
7703	Toss Your Cookies	

7737	Trying To Put A Square Peg In A Round Hole	7770	Two Ships Passing In The Night
7738	Tugging At Heartstrings	7771	Two Sides Of The Same Coin
7739	Tugging At My Heart Strings	7772	Two Thumbs Up
7740	Tune Out	7773	Two Way Street
7741	Turn A New Leaf	7774	Two Wrongs Don't Make A Right
7742	Turn About Is Fair Play		
7743	Turn Back The Clock	7775	Two's Company Three's A Crowd
7744	Turn Back The Hands Of Time	7776	U Is Part Of US
7745	Turn Back The Wheels Of Time	7777	Ugly As A Hat Full Of Holes
		7778	Ugly As A Mud Fence
7746	Turn Coat	7779	Ugly As Sin
7747	Turn On A Dime	7780	Unable To See The Wood For The Trees
7748	Turn On The Heat		
7749	Turn Over A New Leaf	7781	Unbeknownst To Me
7750	Turn The Heat On	7782	Under A Microscope
7751	Turn The Other Cheek	7783	Under Her Thumb
7752	Turn The Page	7784	Under My Skin
7753	Turn The Rascals Out	7785	Under My Wing
7754	Turn The Table	7786	Under The Gun
7755	Turn Up The Heat	7787	Under The Knife
7756	Turning The Corner	7788	Under The Sauce
7757	Tweak Something	7789	Under The Table
7758	Twice As Nice	7790	Under The Weather
7759	Twice As Strong As An Ox And Half As Smart	7791	Under Your Thumb
		7792	Uneasy Lies The Head That Wears The Crown
7760	Twice The Success Half The Effort	7793	Unite And Change The World
7761	Twiddling Your Thumbs	7794	United We Stand Divided We Fall
7762	Twist My Arm		
7763	Twist Of Fate	7795	Unleash The Dragon
7764	Twisting Slowly In The Wind	7796	Unless You Are The Lead Dog The View Never Changes
7765	Two Faced		
7766	Two Heads Are Better Than One	7797	Unlucky At Cards Lucky In Love
7767	Two Is Better Than One	7798	Until The Cows Come Home
7768	Two Left Feet		
7769	Two Of A Kind	7799	Unwind A Deal

137

7800	Up A Creek Without A Paddle
7801	Up For Grabs
7802	Up In Arms
7803	Up In The Air
7804	Up One's Sleeve
7805	Up Shit Creek
7806	Up The Ante
7807	Up The Creek Without A Paddle
7808	Up To His Ears In Trouble
7809	Up To Snuff
7810	Up Your Nose With A Rubber Hose
7811	Up Yours
7812	Uphill Battle
7813	Upper Crust
7814	Upper Handed
7815	Upset The Apple Cart
7816	Use The Force Luke
7817	Useless As Tits On A Boar Hog
7818	Vanity Vanity All Is Vanity
7819	Variety Is The Spice Of Life
7820	Va-Va-Voom
7821	Vengeance Is Sweet
7822	Veni Vidi Vici
7823	Vicious Circle
7824	Victory Has A Hundred Fathers And Defeat Is An Orphan
7825	Viewer Discretion Advised
7826	Virtue Is It's Own Reward
7827	Visa Versa
7828	Viva Las Vegas
7829	Vive la Difference
7830	Waddle On Over
7831	Wait And See
7832	Wait For The Ink To Dry
7833	Wait Till You Hear This

7834	Wait Until You Get Out In The Real World
7835	Wait With Baited Breath
7836	Waiting For The Dust To Settle
7837	Waiting For The Other Shoe To Drop
7838	Waiting For Your Ship To Come In
7839	Waiting In The Wings
7840	Waiting With Baited Breath
7841	Wake Me When It's Over
7842	Wake The Dead
7843	Wake Up
7844	Wake Up And Smell The Butter
7845	Wake Up And Smell The Coffee
7846	Wake Up Call
7847	Waking Up On The Wrong Side Of The Bed
7848	Waking Up With The Chickens
7849	Walk All Over You
7850	Walk In My Shoes
7851	Walk On The Wild Side
7852	Walk Softly And Carry A Big Stick
7853	Walk The Plank
7854	Walk This Way
7855	Walking On Air
7856	Walking On Eggshells
7857	Walking On Sunshine
7858	Walled Garden
7859	Walls Have Ears
7860	Walls Start Closing In
7861	Want A Piece Of Peace
7862	Want My Place In The Sun
7863	Want To Play 52 Pickup
7864	Wanted Dead Or Alive
7865	War Is Hell

138

7866	War Is Too Important To Be Left To The Generals	7898	We Don't Live In A Perfect World
7867	Warm The Cockles Of Your Heart	7899	We Have Met The Enemy And They Are Ours
7868	Wash Your Hands	7900	We Have Nothing To Fear But Fear Itself
7869	Wash Your Mouth Out With Soap	7901	We Just Disagree
7870	Washed Up	7902	We Shall Be Free
7871	Waste Not Want Not	7903	We Shall Overcome
7872	Wasted	7904	We Threw Our Dice Into The Ring And Turned Up Trumps
7873	Watch And Wait		
7874	Watch Me	7905	We Will Proceed On The Assumption That Nothing Will Be Done
7875	Watch My Lips		
7876	Watch The Fur Fly	7906	We Will Rock You
7877	Watch Your Mouth	7907	Wealth Makes Many Friends
7878	Watched Pot Never Boils		
7879	Watching The Clock	7908	Wear Many Hats
7880	Water In The Mouth	7909	Wear Your Heart Out On Your Sleeve
7881	Water Seeks It's Own Level		
7882	Water Water Everywhere But Not A Drop To Drink	7910	Wearing Nothin' But His Birthday Suit
7883	Wave The White Flag	7911	Wearing The Big Girlie Blouse
7884	Way Down Deep He's Shallow	7912	Wearing Your Heart On Your Sleeve
7885	Way To A Man's Heart Is Through His Stomach	7913	Weasel Out Of It
		7914	Weather The Storm
7886	Way To Go	7915	Weep And You'll Weep Alone
7887	Way To Go Einstein		
7888	Way To Go Grace	7916	Welcome To My Hell
7889	We Adopted Him	7917	Welcome To The Club
7890	We Are All In This Together	7918	Welcome To The Jungle
7891	We Are Family	7919	Welcome To the OC Bitch
7892	We Are The Clock Of Time	7920	Welcome To TV Land
7893	We Are The Creators Of Time	7921	We'll Always Have Paris
		7922	We'll Be Right Back
7894	We Are The Killers Of Time	7923	We'll Cross That Bridge When We Come To It
7895	We Are The Victims Of Time		
7896	We Are Two Wild And Crazy Guys	7924	Well Heeled
7897	We Came We Saw We Kicked Ass		

139

7925	Well Here's Another Nice Mess You've Gotten Me Into
7926	Well How Do You Like Them Apples
7927	Well I'll Be A Monkeys Uncle
7928	Well Isn't That Special
7929	We'll Jump That Fence When We Get To It
7930	Well Nobody's Perfect
7931	Well Off
7932	Well That Took The Thunder Out Of His Sails
7933	Well This Is A Fine How Do You Do
7934	Went Belly Up
7935	Went Over Like A Lead Balloon
7936	Went Storming Off In A Huff
7937	Went Through The Roof
7938	We're All In This Together
7939	We're Going To Burn The Midnight Oil
7940	We're Gonna Tie One On Tonight
7941	We're Not In Kansas Anymore
7942	We're Really Goi ng To Town
7943	We're Sitting Ducks
7944	Were You Born In A Barn
7945	Were You Raised By Wolves
7946	Wet Behind The Ears
7947	Wet Blanket
7948	Wet Dream
7949	Wet Your Whistle
7950	We've Got A Really Big Show
7951	We've Hit Pay Dirt
7952	We've Now Come

	Full Circle
7953	Whadaya Hear Whadaya Say
7954	Wham Bam Thank You Mam
7955	Whassup
7956	What A Blast
7957	What A Duck
7958	What A Dump
7959	What A Square
7960	What A Tangled Web We Weave
7961	What A Way To Go
7962	What A Wonderful World
7963	What Am I Chopped Liver
7964	What Are You Chicken
7965	What Are You Driving At
7966	What Are You Stewing About (Over)
7967	What Can't Be Cured Must Be Endured
7968	What Can't Hurt You Can Only Make You Stronger
7969	What Does That Have To Do With The Price Of Tea In China
7970	What Else Can You Do
7971	What Goes Around Comes Around
7972	What Goes Up Must Come Down
7973	What Has Happened Once Can Happen Again
7974	What Have You Done For Me Lately
7975	What I Found Was Shocking
7976	What I Said To Them At Half Time Would Be Unprintable On The Radio
7977	What If This Is As Good As It Gets

7978	What In Tarnation		8005	Whatever Doesn't Kill You Makes You Stronger
7979	What In The Name			
7980	What In The Sam Hill		8006	Whatever Floats Your Boat
7981	What Makes It Tick		8007	Whatever Tickles Your Fancy
7982	What Matters Most			
7983	What Must Be Must Be		8008	Whatever Turns You On
7984	What Now		8009	Whatever You Like
7985	What On Earth Is Wrong With Me		8010	What's A Little Dirt Among Friends
7986	What On Earth Is Wrong With You		8011	What's A Little Quarrel Among Friends
7987	What Part Of No Don't You Understand		8012	What's Cookin' Good Lookin'
7988	What Really Gets Me		8013	What's Done Cannot Be Undone
7989	What Really Happened		8014	What's Done Is Done
7990	What Rock Did You Crawl Out From Under		8015	What's Going Down
7991	What The Dickens		8016	What's Good For The Goose Is Good For The Gander
7992	What The Eye Doesn't See The Heart Doesn't Grieve For			
			8017	What's Happening
7993	What The Heck		8018	What's He Been Smoking
7994	What The Hell Happened To Me		8019	What's In A Name
			8020	What's So Bad About That
7995	What This Country Needs Is A Good 5 Cent Cigar		8021	What's That Got To Do With The Price Of Eggs In Chicago
7996	What To Play Spin The Bottle		8022	What's The Point
			8023	What's The Skinny
7997	What We Have Here Is A Failure To Communicate		8024	What's This Does
			8025	What's Up
7998	What We've Got Here Is A Failure To Communicate		8026	What's Up Doc
			8027	What's Up With That
7999	What Will Be Will Be		8028	What's Wrong With This Picture
8000	What You Do Know Can Hurt You			
			8029	Wheel Is Turning But The Hamster Is Dead
8001	What You Don't Know Can't Hurt You			
			8030	When A Man Loves A Woman
8002	What You See Is What You Get		8031	When All Is Said And Done
8003	What's New Pussycat		8032	When Hell Freezes Over
8004	Whatchoo Talkin About Willis		8033	When I Die

8034	When I Want Your Opinion I'll Give It To You
8035	When I Was His Age
8036	When In Doubt Do Nothing
8037	When In Rome Do As The Romans Do
8038	When It Rains It Pours
8039	When Life Gives You Lemons Make Lemonade
8040	When One Door Closes Another Door Opens
8041	When Pigs Fly
8042	When Pigs Might Fly
8043	When Push Comes To Shove
8044	When The Cat's Away The Mice Will Play
8045	When The Chips Are Down
8046	When The Going Gets Tough The Tough Get Going
8047	When The Levee Breaks
8048	When The Lion Is Dead The Hares Jump On His Back
8049	When The Shit Hits The Fan
8050	When The Student Is Ready The Teacher Will Appear
8051	When The Tide Goes Out The Rocks Begin To Show
8052	When The Work Is Done I Will Have Time For Myself
8053	When Times Get Rough
8054	When Will I Be Loved
8055	When X Speaks Y Listens
8056	When You Believe
8057	When You Come To The Fork In The Road Take It
8058	When You Got It Flaunt It
8059	When You Lie With Dogs You Catch Fleas

8060	When You Start Picking Out People You Start Leaving People Out
8061	Whenever I Look For Something It's Always In The Last Place I Look
8062	Where Are The Snows Of Yesteryear
8063	Where Do I Begin
8064	Where Do We Go From Here
8065	Where Do You Draw The Line
8066	Where The Rubber Meets The Road
8067	Where There's A Will There's A Way
8068	Where There's Life There's Hope
8069	Where There's No Vision The People Perish
8070	Where There's Smoke There's Fire
8071	Where You Are
8072	Where's The Beef
8073	Wherever You Go There You Are
8074	Whew
8075	Which Came First The Chicken Or The Egg
8076	While Away The Hours
8077	While The Tailor Rests The Needle Rusts
8078	While These Results May Seem Rather Trivial Their Importance Cannot Be Underestimated
8079	Whipper Snapper
8080	Whipping Boy
8081	Whistle Down The Wind
8082	Whistle While You Work
8083	Whistling In The Dark

8084	White As A Sheet
8085	White Collar Worker
8086	White Elephant
8087	White Knuckle Ride
8088	White Man Speak With Forked Tongue
8089	White Room
8090	Who Could Forget
8091	Who Died And Left You In Charge
8092	Who Died And Made Him King
8093	Who Died And Made You King
8094	Who Just Cut The Cheese
8095	Who Knew
8096	Who Let The Dogs Out
8097	Who Loves You Baby
8098	Who Pissed In Your Cheerios
8099	Who Was That Masked Man
8100	Who's Cryin' Now
8101	Who's Sorry Now
8102	Whoever Dies With The Most Toys Wins
8103	Whole Enchilada
8104	Whole Kit And Kaboodle
8105	Whole Lotta Love
8106	Whole Nine Yards
8107	Whole Shootin' Match
8108	Who'll Stop The Rain
8109	Whoop It Up
8110	Who's On First
8111	Who's That Knockin' At My Door
8112	Who's The Man
8113	Who's Your Go To Guy
8114	Whose Bread I Eat His Song I Sing
8115	Whose Counting
8116	Whose Minding The Store

8117	Whose Your Daddy
8118	Why Bad Things Happen To Good Websites
8119	Why Buy The Cow When The Milk Is Free
8120	Why Close The Barn Door After The Horse Is Gone
8121	Why Do Today What You Can Put Off 'Til Tomorrow
8122	Why Do You Have To Make Everything So Difficult
8123	Why Don't We All Chip In
8124	Why Don't You Come Up See Me Sometime
8125	Why On God's Green Earth
8126	Wide Open Spaces
8127	Wig Out
8128	Wild Goose Chase
8129	Wild Thing
8130	Will Miracles Never Cease
8131	Will Wonders Never Cease
8132	Willy Nilly
8133	Win Hands Down
8134	Win One For The Gipper
8135	Win Some Lose Some
8136	Win Win
8137	Windjammer
8138	Wing It
8139	Winging It
8140	Winkin Blinkin And Nod
8141	Winners Never Quit And Quitters Never Win
8142	Winning Combination
8143	Winning Isn't Everything It's The Only Thing
8144	Wins Hands Down
8145	Wipe That Smile Off Your Face
8146	Wipe The Slate Clean
8147	Wise For His Age
8148	Wish Bone

143

8149	Wish Upon A Star
8150	Wish You Were Here
8151	Wishy Washy
8152	Witch Hunt
8153	With A Fine Tooth Comb
8154	With A Grain Of Salt
8155	With A High Hand
8156	With Arms Wide Open
8157	With Credit Cards Eagerly In Hand
8158	With Malice Toward None With Charity For All
8159	With One Hand Tied Behind My Back
8160	With Success Comes Prosperity
8161	With Such Friends One Hardly Needs Enemies
8162	With The Click Of A Mouse
8163	With The Greatest Of Ease
8164	With Tongue Firmly Planted In Cheek
8165	With Your Tail Between Your Legs
8166	Within An Ace Of
8167	Without Rhyme Or Reason
8168	Withstand The Test Of Time
8169	Wolf In Sheep's Clothing
8170	Women And Children First
8171	Won't Make The Cut
8172	Won't Work A Lick
8173	Word Of Mouth
8174	Word On The Street
8175	Words Once Spoken You Can Never Recall
8176	Work At Home
8177	Work Half As Much The Total Result Would Be The Same
8178	Work Hard Play Hard

8179	Work In A Vacuum
8180	Work Into A Lather
8181	Work Like A Dog
8182	Work Never Hurt Anybody
8183	Work Out All The Kinks
8184	Work Smart
8185	Work Smart And Attract Partners
8186	Work The Crowd
8187	Work The Room
8188	Work Your Fingers To The Bone
8189	Worked Night And Day
8190	Worked To Death
8191	Worker Bee
8192	Working From The Bottom Up
8193	Working My Last Good Nerve
8194	Works For Me
8195	Works His But Off
8196	Works Like Clockwork
8197	World Is Your Oyster
8198	World Of Hurt
8199	World Of Trouble
8200	World On A String
8201	World Weary
8202	Worm Has Turned
8203	Worry Wart
8204	Worth His Weight In Gold
8205	Worth His Weight In Salt
8206	Worth Its Weight In Gold
8207	Worthless As Tits On A Boar
8208	Would You Believe
8209	Would You Buy A Used Car From This Man
8210	Wouldn't Kick Him Outta Bed For Eatin' Crackers
8211	Wound Tight As A Drum
8212	Wound Tighter Than A

144

	Spring
8213	Wreak Havoc
8214	Write This Down
8215	Writing's On The Wall
8216	Wrong End Of The Stick
8217	Wrong Side Of The Bed
8218	Wrong Side Of The Tracks
8219	X Marks The Spot
8220	Yabba Dabba Do
8221	Yada Yada Yada
8222	Yank Your Chain
8223	Yard Arm
8224	Yeah Baby Yeah
8225	Yeah That's The Ticket
8226	Year In And Year Out
8227	Yes Virginia There Is A Santa Claus
8228	Yester Year
8229	You Ain't Seen Nada Yet
8230	You Ain't Seen Nothing Yet
8231	You Are So Beautiful
8232	You Are What You Eat
8233	You Bet Your Boots
8234	You Better Believe It
8235	You Can Bank On It
8236	You Can Catch More Flies With Honey Than With Vinegar
8237	You Can Dish It Out But You Can't Take It
8238	You Can Fool Some Of The People Some Of The Time
8239	You Can Hear A Pin Drop
8240	You Can Lead A Horse To Water But You Can't Make Him Drink
8241	You Can Lead A Horticulture But You Can't Make It Think
8242	You Can Never Be Too Rich Or Too Blonde

8243	You Can Never Go Home Again
8244	You Can Pick Your Friends And You Can Pick Your Nose
8245	You Can Run But You Can't Hide
8246	You Can Say That Again
8247	You Can Take That To The Bank
8248	You Can Take The Boy Out Of The Country But
8249	You Can Tell The Men From The Boys By The Price Of Their Toys
8250	You Cannot Judge Someone Until You Have Walked A Mile In Their Shoes
8251	You Can't Argue With Success
8252	You Can't Beat A Man At His Own Game
8253	You Can't Believe A Liar When He Tells The Truth
8254	You Can't Fight City Hall
8255	You Can't Fit A Round Peg Into A Square Hole
8256	You Can't Fit A Square Peg In A Round Hole
8257	You Can't Get Blood From A Stone
8258	You Can't Go Home Again
8259	You Can't Handle The Truth
8260	You Can't Have It Both Ways
8261	You Can't Have Your Cake And Eat It Too
8262	You Can't Hurry Love
8263	You Can't Judge A Book By Its Cover

145

8264	You Can't Learn To Swim Without Getting Into The Water
8265	You Can't Live With Men And You Can't Live Without Them
8266	You Can't Lose What You Never Had
8267	You Can't Make A Silk Purse Out Of A Sow's Ear
8268	You Can't Make An Omelet Without Breaking Eggs
8269	You Can't Please Everyone
8270	You Can't Please Your Honey Without Any Money
8271	You Can't Put Anything Past Her
8272	You Can't Put The Toothpaste Back In The Tube
8273	You Can't Say Enough About Him
8274	You Can't Squeeze Blood Out Of A Turnip
8275	You Can't Step Twice Into The Same River
8276	You Can't Stop Him You Can Only Hope To Contain Him
8277	You Can't Swing A Dead Cat
8278	You Can't Take It With You
8279	You Can't Take Knickers Off A Bare Arse
8280	You Can't Take That Away From Me
8281	You Can't Teach An Old Dog New Tricks
8282	You Can't Unscramble Eggs
8283	You Can't Win Them All
8284	You Complete Me

8285	You Could Have Knocked Me Over With A Feather
8286	You Could Hear A Pin Drop
8287	You Could Knock Me Over With A Feather
8288	You Could Put Your Eye Out
8289	You Deserve The Very Best
8290	You Do Wonders In Your Pants
8291	You Don't Know What Love Is
8292	You Don't Get Something For Nothing
8293	You Don't Have A Leg To Stand On
8294	You Don't Have To Spin Hay Into Gold
8295	You Don't Miss The Water Till The Well Runs Dry
8296	You Don't Think So Eh That's Your Trouble You Don't Think
8297	You Drive Me Crazy
8298	You Drive Me Nuts
8299	You Drive Me Up A Wall
8300	You Eeeediot
8301	You Get What You Pay For
8302	You Go Girl
8303	You Go To My Head
8304	You Got It Coming To You
8305	You Got Just What You Deserve
8306	You Got That Right Pilgrim
8307	You Got Your Just Reward
8308	You Gotta Do What You Gotta Do
8309	You Gotta Put Your Foot Down
8310	You Had Me At Hello
8311	You Have A Right To Be Skeptical

146

8312	You Have One Choice
8313	You Have The Distinction Of Being The Only One Who Is Not Exceptional
8314	You Have To Break A Few Eggs To Make An Omelet
8315	You Have To Eat All Your Food Before You Get Dessert
8316	You Have To Learn To Crawl Before You Can Walk
8317	You Have To Play The Hand You're Dealt
8318	You Have To See It To Believe It
8319	You Have To Separate The Chaff From The Wheat
8320	You Have To Stand For Something Or You'll Fall For Anything
8321	You Have To Take The Bitter With The Sweet
8322	You Hit The Nail On The Head
8323	You Just Missed Him
8324	You Know Better Than That
8325	You Lie Like A Dog
8326	You Lie Like A Rug
8327	You Look Like Death Warmed Over
8328	You Look Mahvelous
8329	You Lost Me
8330	You Made Your Bed Now Your Gonna Have To Lie In It
8331	You Make A Better Door Than A Window
8332	You Make Me Feel So Young
8333	You Make Me Want To Be A Better Man
8334	You Make The Call
8335	You Must Be Out Of

	Your Mind
8336	You Must Crawl Before You Can Walk
8337	You Must Row With The Oars That You Have
8338	You Name It We Have It
8339	You Never Had It So Good
8340	You Never Know A Man Until You Live With Him
8341	You Never Miss The Water Till The Well Runs Dry
8342	You Only Hurt The One You Love
8343	You Only Live Once
8344	You Poop It You Scoop It
8345	You Rang
8346	You Really Blow Me Away
8347	You Reap What You Sow
8348	You Said It
8349	You Say Potato I Say Pahtato
8350	You Scratch My Back And I'll Scratch Yours
8351	You Shall Reap What You Sow
8352	You Simply Won't Believe It
8353	You Snooze You Loose
8354	You Still Turn Me On
8355	You Take The High Road And I'll Take The Low Road
8356	You Talkin' To Me
8357	You Throw Filth On The Living And Flowers On The Dead
8358	You Took Advantage Of Me
8359	You Turned The Tables On Me
8360	You Wash My Back I'll Wash Yours
8361	You Were The Gleam In Your Father's Eye

147

8362	You Win Some You Lose Some
8363	You'll Be Damned If You Do And Damned If You Don't
8364	You'll Have To Pinch Yourself
8365	You'll Know It When You See It
8366	You'll Never Be Disappointed Expecting Nothing
8367	You'll Never Get Out Alive
8368	You'll Never Know Unless You Try
8369	You'll Regret It
8370	Young & Foolish
8371	Your Dumb & Full Of Rum
8372	Young Loins
8373	Your Ass Is Grass
8374	Your Barking Up The Wrong Tree
8375	Your Barn Door's Open
8376	Your Call Cannot Be Completed As Dialed
8377	Your Cheatin' Heart
8378	Your Eyes Are Too Big For Your Stomach
8379	Your Father Wasn't A Glass Maker
8380	Your Goose Is Cooked
8381	Your Guess Is As Good As Mine
8382	Your Mother's Uncle
8383	Your Official Kick In The Butt
8384	Your Place Or Mine
8385	Your Rich Uncle
8386	Your Wish Is Our Command
8387	You're A Good Egg
8388	You're A Hottie

8389	You're About As Useful As A Poopie Flavored Lollipop
8390	You're All Wet Behind The Ears
8391	You're Already Here
8392	You're Breaking My Heart
8393	You're Dead Meat
8394	You're Driving Me Insane
8395	You're Fired
8396	You're Going To Get It
8397	You're Gonna Need A Bigger Boat
8398	You're Hot
8399	You're In Big Trouble Mister
8400	You're In Or You're Dead It's Your Choice
8401	You're In The Money
8402	You're It
8403	You're Just Seconds Away
8404	You're Leaving Money On The Table
8405	You're My Knight In Shinning Armor
8406	You're Never Too Old To Learn
8407	You're No Good
8408	You're Not Going To Believe This
8409	You're Not Too Smart Are You
8410	You're Off Your Rocker
8411	You're Out
8412	You're Pulling My Leg
8413	You're Really Beginning To Piss Me Off
8414	You're So Vain
8415	You're Still The One
8416	You're The Bee's Knees
8417	You're The Boss

148

8418	You're The Disease And I'm The Cure		8431	You've Got Nerve
8419	You're The Gleam In Your Father's Eye		8432	You've Got Nothing To Lose And Everything To Gain
8420	You're The Love Of My Life		8433	You've Got Spunk
8421	You're The Man		8434	You've Got To Come Back A Star
8422	You're The One That I Want		8435	You've Got To Start Somewhere
8423	You're Why Cavemen Chiseled On Walls		8436	You've Lost That Lovin' Feelin'
8424	Yours Mine And Ours		8437	You've Made Your Bed Now Lie In It
8425	Youth Will Be Served		8438	You've Outdone Yourself As Usual
8426	Youth Will Have It's Fling		8439	Zero Tolerance
8427	You've Come A Long Way Baby		8440	Zigged When He Should Have Zagged
8428	You've Got An Open Invitation		8441	Zip Your Lips
8429	You've Got Mail			
8430	You've Got More Front Than Myers			

The Cliché Bible

8,400 Great Clichés For Sports Fanatics & Lovers Of Popular Expressions.

Well, hopefully these should keep you at the top of your lingo game. And YES, after much discussion, we felt it imporant to include variations of the same Cliché in order to help all of our readers find them faster.

If you have a great Cliché you feel we've missed but deserve to be included, ommitted, or corrected in our upcoming publications, please consider sending us an email update at: (support@RIVOinc.com). Please keep all suggestions relatively adult & kid friendly.

We truly appreciate your support and look forward to hearing from you.

Richard & Lynn Voigt

About The Authors:

Richard and Lynn help clients clarify their talents and develop creative strategies that paint dreams, sell ideas, and market messages. They help everyday people create an action plan that discovers and connects the missing pieces of a client's success puzzle.

Together, they present a unique team-approach with each client, working side-by-side; utilizing their life-long skills and diverse expertise as education specialists, Internet marketers, entrepreneurs, inventors, artists, authors, and life & business coaches,.

Teaching by example, they focus on proven systems, research and development, trends & technology, key domain portfolio acquisitions, video production, self-publishing, along with managing over a hundred of premium keyword websites on behalf of their company, RIVO Inc – RIVO Marketing.

Their life-long mission is to continually uncover brand new strategies, products, and services, networking useful solutions for their clients, online & offline entrepreneurs, small business owners, writers, local artists, models, teachers, and students and marketing professionals.

Feel free to contact them if you have questions or would like to tap into their talents and expertise. They would appreciate your feedback and success stories.

Richard & Lynn Voigt - RIVO
I. M. Education Specialists

RIVO INC - RIVO Marketing
Website: www.RIVOinc.com
Email: support@RIVOinc.com
Want To See What We've Been Up To:

Visit Lynn's Garden: www.WisconsinGarden.net
view hundreds of great garden video blogs

See Richard's Unique Artwork: www.RIVOart.com
view over 3,000 original compositions

Additional RIVO Titles Now On Amazon:

The CLICHÉ BIBLE - 8,400 Cliches For Sports Fanatics & Lovers Of PopularExpresssions

The Golden Vault Of Motivational Quotations –
Words of Wisdom From The Greatest Minds & Leaders

ACTION HEADLINES That Drive Emotions – Volumes 1- 6
Paint Dreams, Sell Ideas & Market Your Message

BABY NAME.me – 21,400+ Baby Names & Nicknames –
For Family, Friends, Pets, Natural & Man-Objects

DOODLE DESIGNS Volume 1 & 2
For Professionals & Kids Of All Ages

DOODLE DESIGN Coloring Book
For Professionals & Kids Of All Ages

PERSONAL NOTES: